Baseball's Starry Night

Reliving Major League Baseball's 2011
Wild Card Night of Shock and Awe

Paul Kocak

digitature

ISBN-13: 978-0615622309
ISBN-10: 0615622305

Cover Art: Ethan Kocak
Cover Design & Layout: Connor Raus
Author Photo: Adrianna Kocak

Digitature
118 Waverly Place
New York, New York 10011
http://www.digitature.com

To Beth,
without whom…
and to Ethan, Evelyn, and Adrianna

Foreword

So I get a phone call at 12:21 a.m. in March from someone I have never met but feel I have known for years. It's Lenn Fraraccio, known on Twitter as @RaysFanGio. He is calling from Florida, all excited, talking baseball. Talking baseball at the end of winter in Syracuse, New York, is mighty fine with me, but at 12:21 a.m.? Lenn, or more precisely "Gio," his uber-intense baseball persona, is calling to talk with me once again about the after-effects of Game 162 of 2011.

OK. Talk to me, Gio.

The subject is painful for Red Sox and Braves followers. And it is a delightful memory for Cardinals and Rays fans. For Rays fans like Gio, the aura of September 28, 2011 will never fade. But for baseball fans like me, and legions of fans of other teams, our memory of that evening of baseball is more like: What was that all about? Did you see that? How could it have ended that way? And, most of all: where were you when all that was going on?

Baseball is a metaphor for the future. And it's a metaphor for the past, too. Speaking of remembering, remember when baseball had two leagues with eight teams and there was none of this "wild card" business? Those were the days when "wild card" only referred to poker or gin rummy or crazy behavior of one of the guys in the Gashouse Gang. Baseball lived in a purer, simpler time.

And what about the future? Baseball is a metaphor for homogenized branding, corporate welfare, and commercial infiltration. By the time you are reading this, players' uniforms might have logos and microchips sending subliminal messages to fans to buy coffee, beer, or condoms.

That's why September 28, 2011, is such an epochal date on the calendar. Baseball will never and can never be the same after that date. Why? Because Major League Baseball is headed toward inter-league play all the time anytime. Now MLB will have a play-in game for (wait for it) the Wild Card. September 28 is Fulcrum Day. Circle THAT on your calendar. It's the day at a pivotal point between the past and the future. The stars will never align like they did on that night. Never again. The baseball gods and goddesses will not allow that. And neither will baseball's military-industrial-mega-corporate complex.

But baseball is a mirror as well as a metaphor machine.

The mirror on that night was a mirror of collapse and comeback.

Why did the Boston Red Sox and the Atlanta Braves collapse? The reasons are complex. People will speculate for years. Who knows? In a December 2011 animated (would any other kind be possible?) phone conversation about that night with former Major League pitcher Bill "Spaceman" Lee, he mentioned that he happened to have been reading *Collapse* by Jared Diamond just before the monumental collapses of those teams. He said he was not too surprised. So I too took a look at that excellent book. (Diamond, it turns out, is reportedly a Red Sox fan.) You can see collapse coming if you look at the signs.

Baseball has its own ecosystem, just like societies and tribes and civilizations do. Those teams collapsed just like the people on Easter Island in the Pacific Ocean pretty much disappeared, just like the Anasazi tribe in America's Southwest went extinct, just like the celebrated Mayan civilization fell apart after its glory days (to use a Bruce Springsteen song title). Another example is the Norse people in Greenland, who could not survive, although the Inuit did. These societies plundered their environments, looked at the immediate gain, and disregarded the long term.

Diamond says about kings and nobles: "Their attention was evidently focused on their short-term concerns of enriching themselves, waging wars, erecting monuments, competing with each other, and extracting enough food from the peasants to support all those activities." [p. 177]. Sound familiar? Translate "kings and nobles" to Major League Baseball owners. Better yet, for the sake of argument, let's translate to "Boston Red Sox." Before the 2011 season, they signed Carl Crawford for seven years at $142 million. (Oh, by the way, he used to be on the Tampa Bay Rays. Crawford was both their "sparkplug and distributor," to use Bill Lee's analogy. A taste of karma, anyone?) And when it mattered the most, when a sinking liner in Baltimore was headed toward Carl Crawford, he was in the wrong place at the wrong time. He did a reverse-retro-anti-karma-semi-quasi-counter-subjunctive Willie Mays. The Catch became the Uncatch. The Yes! became the Oh-no! And why was Mr. Crawford in the wrong place at the wrong time? To be fair to him, forces beyond his control did not help. Remember that 2011 was a year of catastrophic earthquakes. A 9.0 quake on March 11 off the coast of Japan and the resulting tsunami killed tens of thousands of people – and changed the axis of the planet! Japan moved. And if Japan moves, so does left field at Oriole Park at Camden Yards in Baltimore. Crawford was not sensitive to that infinitesimal adjustment. Wrong place at the wrong time. Maybe if he had regularly walked to work, as did second baseman Dustin Pedroia, who lived minutes from Fenway Park, he would've been more attuned to the cosmic forces. But we can't just single him out. Red Sox closer Jonathan Papelbon was insensitive to the same forces as he let the game slip away like sand in an hourglass in the bottom of the ninth inning to see the hopes of the Red Sox evaporate like the radioactive cloud above Fukishima II in Japan.

And speaking of monuments of civilizations, this was the same year that an earthquake damaged the Washington Monument and the National Cathedral in Washington, D.C., in August, not that terribly far from Camden Yards. (As The Spaceman (Bill Lee) once reportedly noted, "You should enter a ballpark the way you enter a church." They are both sacred spaces.) If you recall the 1989 World Series between the San Francisco Giants and Oakland A's, you will understand how an earthquake can directly affect baseball.

Even though manager Terry Francona lost his job over the Red Sox' collapse, let's just say, "It was written," as The Spaceman suggested. It was destined to happen. As with the collapsing Polynesian societies or the Scandinavians in Greenland described by Jared Diamond, the conditions for doom were ripe. The

Red Sox and their fans did not know what hit them. (Well, they did, actually. Those dour, hard-bitten Puritans of New England are always under a pall, expecting doom and divine judgment. It's in the air. It's part of their history.)

And what about history? The year 2011 was not a benchmark of collaboration and coexistence, was it? Heck, the so-called leaders of our government played chicken with each other and almost let the government shut down as they argued about money, just like a bitter, old married couple.

What can we say about the collapse of the Atlanta Braves? That one is harder to figure out. Did their young pitchers simply run out of gas? Hard to say. Did the Braves miss Bobby Cox? Maybe. I'll try this: The Atlanta Braves lost on September 28, 2011, and for large swaths of September, because of bad karma related to their long-ago departure from Boston. Remember that the Boston Braves became the Milwaukee Braves became the Atlanta Braves. Maybe they should have remained loyal to Boston and stayed there. On the other hand, maybe it's some sort of payback for their name and the tomahawk chop and all that. I'm just throwing that out there; it might be a little outrageous and cannot be proved. But that's never stopped me before from offering an opinion.

As I said, baseball is not just a mirror of collapse. It's also a mirror of comeback and triumph, unlike any other sport, really. And that's the fun part. That's the cosmic fireworks. What about the Cardinals and the Rays? What about them indeed? The St. Louis Cardinals, under manager Tony LaRussa, were what you would expect from a team smack-dab in the middle of the country. Their Midwestern, Lutheran virtues of perseverance and hope paid off. Their flannel-shirted steadiness proved that playing hard against all odds sometimes exceeds all expectations – even your own. Their victory on September 28 could not be celebrated just by themselves; they needed a little help from the team in the City of Brotherly Love and they needed to take care of business down in Houston town, which they did in business-like fashion. Think of George Bailey in "It's a Wonderful Life" and you have your 2011 St. Louis Cardinals.

If that is true of the Cardinals, what of the Tampa Bay Rays? Let's face it, they and their fans are the emotional heroes of our story. Not just because of timing and not just because the Rays and their fans were Act V in a Shakespearean comedy (tragedy, for Red Sox Nation). You can't make up what they did! It's like Sonny Liston coming up off the mat and knocking out Cassius Clay! With manager Joe Maddon making magical moves that defied what "the book" called for, he became the Duke of Wellington

in Belgium in June of 1815. His flexibility, his
looseness, and his intuition – above all, his belief in
his men – paid off. Just as the Battle of Waterloo
remains etched in history as the downfall of Napoleon,
so the Rays victory on this starry night will always
stand as one of the great comebacks, with the
combatants in this case going by names like Evan
Longoria and Dan Johnson.

To spice up our story, we have the almighty Yankees
losing no sleep over seeing the Red Sox crumble, even
if it meant the Yankees shamefully blew a seven-run
lead. Nor did the Phillies cry as they nipped their
National League East rivals, the Braves, to deny them.
We have under-sub-underdogs like the Baltimore
Orioles and Houston Astros playing supporting roles.
In fact, the Orioles' one victory that night looked as if
they had won the darned World Series.

The moral of the story is this: we the fans got to
experience an unfolding and then catalytic drama that
glorified our sport, wherever we were. Whether it was
agony or ecstasy, we said to one another, "Can you
believe this?"

Here's hoping you find this chronicle both
entertaining and rewarding. I invite you to relive this
singular night, whether it was a painful memory or a
jubilant one. Whether you witnessed it then or are

experiencing it here for the first time through the prism of fans' passions, grab some peanuts and popcorn for four games for the ages for all true baseball fans.

P.S. Sweet dreams to Gio and all citizens of Die-hard Fans Nation.

Paul Kocak
Syracuse, New York
March 8, 2012

Chapter 1
A Night of Shooting Stars

Horatio:
O day and night, but this is wondrous strange!

Hamlet:
And therefore as a stranger give it welcome.
There are more things in heaven and earth, Horatio,
Than are dreamt of in your philosophy.

Hamlet, Act 1, Scene 5
William Shakespeare

Help me out here. September 28, 2011. Was this date circled on your calendar? Did Nostradamus prophesy anything about it in 1555? Did astrophysicist-Sabermetricians calculate that on this day the torsional forces of the Earth would align with the polar reversal of tectonic plates and magma tides so that karmic electromagnetic fields produced the wackiest night in baseball history?

We were unprepared for this. Sure, any fans gathered at Stonehenge smugly knew. But what about the rest of us fans, the couch-sitting, potato-chip chomping, bleacher-beer-swilling kind? Nobody warned the loyal legions of Red Sox Nation or the tomahawk-chopping followers of the Atlanta Braves. And only the most stubbornly hopeful cheerleaders of the Saint Louis Cardinals or Tampa Bay Rays saw this night as anything more than an irrational wish.

Irrational narrative. Against all odds. Poetic. Tragic unraveling. Soaring triumph. Take your pick.

Who saw it coming?

No baseball seer predicted this jigsaw puzzle. Cardinals proudly flapping human wings after Chris Carpenter fields J.D. Martinez's weak grounder for the final out of a complete-game victory in Houston. The vanguished Braves' Dan Uggla on his knees and Freddie Freeman's head in his hands in Atlanta. One infinitely tiny baseball eluding a sliding Carl Crawford, puncturing the hope of Red Sox Nation. And Tampa Bay's Evan Longoria reincarnating Bobby Thomson at the Trop by swatting a home run that completed the celestial dance.

What happened here?

Four games were played. Nothing special about that. But in a rapid-fire series of stunning reversals, the baseball season of 2011 closed with cymbals and cannons and fireworks. And when the smoke cleared, the losers as well as victors hardly knew what hit them.

The world had its daily share of distractions and disasters. Worries over a second bailout of Greece sent the Dow Jones Industrial Average down 179.79 points, to 11,010.10 (such portentous numerals!). This was after the DJIA had gained 413 points the previous two days. The FBI had arrested a 26-year-old American, alleging he was plotting to fly remote-controlled planes with explosives into the Pentagon and the Capitol. American soldiers were dying in Iraq and Afghanistan. Infected cantaloupes from Colorado were said to have caused 13 death and 72 illnesses in 18 states from listeriosis. Boeing's 787 Dreamliner arrived in Tokyo on its maiden voyage. Earlier in the year, an Arab Spring of political upheavals.

Four games. One night. For all the marbles. Or at least enough marbles to keep from going home for the winter.

Saint Louis Cardinals at Houston Astros
The Cardinals erased a 10½-game deficit on Aug. 25 to overtake the Braves on the last day of the 2011 regular season. For that to happen, they had to win

and the Atlanta Braves had to lose on the last day. The Cardinals did their part by defeating the Houston Astros 8-0. In a remarkable surge, the Redbirds had won 23 of their last 31 regular-season games. The first piece of the crucial turn of Rubik's Cube was in position.

Atlanta Braves at Philadelphia Phillies
The Braves' heretofore sensational rookie closer Craig Kimbrel surrendered the tying run in the ninth, and the Philadelphia Phillies beat Atlanta 4-3 in the bottom of the thirteenth inning with two outs to end Atlanta's season without advancing to the playoffs – something that seemed certain a few weeks before. The Braves had been up by 8½ games on the morning of September 6.

Boston Red Sox at Baltimore Orioles
With a stunning two-run ninth inning, the Baltimore Orioles rallied to overcome Boston 4-3, setting the stage for eliminating the Red Sox from postseason play minutes later. Red Sox closer Jonathan Papelbon struck out the first two batters before giving up two doubles followed by a single to left that eluded a sliding Carl Crawford. Boston had held a nine-game lead in the AL wild-card race after Sept. 3, but a 7-19 September swoon left them tied with Tampa Bay entering the final day of the regular season. Boston became the first team to miss the postseason after

leading by as many as nine games for a playoff spot entering September, according to the Elias Sports Bureau. Boston's 7-20 mark matched its worst record for a September.

New York Yankees at Tampa Bay Rays

Minutes after the meltdown of the Red Sox, the Tampa Bay Rays surged from a 7-0 deficit with a startling 8-7 win over the New York Yankees in 12 innings. The Rays' improbable comeback climaxed with Evan Longoria's second home run of the game, giving the Rays the AL wild card. Earlier, a hunch by Rays Manager Joe Maddon paid off when pinch hitter Dan Johnson, batting a paltry .108, connected with a two-out, two-strike solo home run in the ninth to tie the game at seven runs apiece. Longoria's blast came just after midnight in the East, roughly four minutes after Boston's loss.

In South Carolina, Yankees fan Denis Ray checked out four TVs, while Pat Driscoll one street away from me in Syracuse watched on a quad screen. In Saint Louis, longtime Cardinals fans Chris and Shellie Hexter high-tenned and jumped up and down in their living room. As reported in the then-St. Petersburg Times, "In Tampa, Carlos Borges and his wife went into the garage to watch the game on their laptop, instead of on the TV inside. Something good, they thought, was about to happen. They didn't want to wake up their sleeping kids."

Even if your team was not involved, you knew something special was in the air. Maybe those Mayan doomsayers were onto something with their ominous talk of the orbit of Comet Elenin (a.k.a. Planet X or Nibiru). (But, truth be told, they were all hot and bothered about September 27, 2011, until the next eschatological prediction came along.)

America loves underdogs. Does that romance hearken back to our Revolutionary origins as colonial upstarts? Or perhaps it reinforces egalitarian notions of justice and comeuppance. We love the long shot – sometimes grudgingly, especially if we are on the predicted losing end. The brash twenty-two-year-old Cassius Clay surprising Sonny Liston in 1964, the Miracle Mets taking the World Series in 1969, and Seabiscuit outrunning War Admiral in 1938 are but a few of the underdog triumphs in American sports. But rarely do underdog triumphs commingle as they did on the night of September 28, 2011. Rarely do the mighty fall so far so fast so simultaneously (loss being the inevitable back of the same coin of triumph) as they did on that same autumn evening. Rarely do we get treated to two colossal collapses merging with two equally ferocious comebacks. Various sports information outlets framed the time

span of excitement: 89 minutes being ESPN Stats
and Information's window, and 129 minutes the
markers for *Sports Illustrated*. Tom Verducci of *Sports
Illustrated* wrote, "They will go down as the most
thrilling 129 minutes in baseball history." A
comprehensive 2011 year-end story by Lee Jenkins in
Sports Illustrated flatly declared September 28 the
"Best. Night. Ever" in its title, and went on to share
game highlights and insider anecdotes. Whatever
minutes you wanted to focus on, depending on how
you calibrated the Cooperstownian seismo-chrono-
graphs, baseball would dance its most thrilling ballet,
with choreography not by George Balanchine but by
the likes of Joe Maddon and Terry Francona, Buck
Showalter and Joe Girardi, Fredi Gonzalez and
Charlie Manuel. From the first pitches at 7:10 p.m.
in Atlanta and Baltimore to the last swing in St.
Petersburg at 12:05 a.m., the axis of the sport tilted.
Featuring rain delays that merely advanced the sense
of dull inevitability, the scoreboard lights displayed
seemingly safe leads (7-0 after seven innings) and
logically assured endings (two strikes with two outs,
more than once).

Personal confession: Since I am not a clairvoyant, on
that Wednesday evening in September 2011 I was a
fairly disengaged fan. My team, the San Francisco
Giants, had been eliminated from postseason
contention in their year of World Championship

basking. At the terminus of this season's ride, another team would claim the crown. Earlier in the evening I was hanging out — if that is what reading and posting blog comments can be called — at Oneflapdown77.com, a blog for San Francisco Giants fans, affectionately known as The Flap. It was a singular pleasure to meet the blog's owner and founder just before Game 1 of the 2010 World Series in San Francisco. (Yes, I went out there without having tickets or a realistic chance of scoring any.) As happens in the virtual world these days, I was also following the course of all the Game 162s via Internet pitch-by-pitch updates, in this case provided by ESPN.com. On top of that, I was alternately pretending to be working and emailing baseball friends and others. My niece emailed me a photo of her and Darryl Strawberry from the finale at CitiField in Flushing, New York. If you want to know the shameful, unbaseballish truth, fellow Flap blogger Steve Melikean, from Colorado, and I were trading emails about palindromes. He bested me and closed off that topic by sending me a computer-generated, allegedly longest palindrome, quickly followed by a long, complex-looking palindrome in Sanskrit. (Palindromes in Sanskrit! That explains what would unfold on this night!) Along the way, we exchanged a few baseball notes about the games in progress, such as, "come on Rays! they were down 7-0!!" as the underdogs showed signs of growling. But when Steve

emailed me the simple message "cha ching . . . tied" I
knew what he meant, signed off, and ran downstairs
to watch on our family television. From there, I was
enthralled. I woke up the next day saying, "Somebody
should write a book about this."

You knew this would be the topic at work tomorrow,
if you had a job. For some, it would be too painful to
discuss. A knowing nod and bloodshot eyes would say
it all: "This one is going to hurt for a long, long time."
And for others, the shared smile, or exclamation-
riddled email, would translate to one word:
"Unbelievable."

Chapter 2
That's Why They Call It the Wild Card

"For social scientists, experiments are like
microscopes or strobe lights. They help us slow
human behavior to a frame-by-frame narration of
events…"

- Dan Ariely, *Predictably Irrational*

Baseball is a team marathon combined with a
thousand individual sprints. The long-distance run to
the postseason begins in February, in Arizona or
Florida warmth, while much of the rest of the nation
is shivering. By the end of March or early April, the
162 games that count begin, stretching to the end of
September or early October. It's a long day's journey
into many night games and endless flights. The
regular season's marathon tests players and fans alike.
Hope soars and recedes. Surprises both tragic and
triumphant are inevitable. And the sprints of
individual performance, from batting streaks to games

saved to errorless chances, figure into a cosmic
equation that no one has figured out yet. So, if your
team is left standing on the last day of the season, it's
a testament to endurance, skill, and a little bit of luck.
Being alive on the last day of the season keeps the last
embers of hope warm, sometimes to the surprise of
everyone – even those who confidently predicted sure
failure, or even success, back in the sunny spring. It is
inevitably a day that looks backwards as well as
forwards, as if standing on a peak. "We've made it.
We can keep going," is something that all players,
coaches, managers, owners, and loyal fans dream of
until mathematics rules such declarations null and
void.

The enterprise of Major League Baseball in modern
America has thirty teams. As of 2011, only eight
teams got to keep playing after the regular season,
making Major League Baseball among the purest
sports in America's vast and expensive landscape of
athletic entertainment.

In 2011, on Wednesday, September 28, the last day
of the Major League Baseball season, much had
already been decided. In many respects, the season's
pennant races had been devoid of any great suspense
or drama. The Detroit Tigers took the AL Central –
the first AL Central crown for the Tigers – on
September 16 (its first division title since 1987), easily

beating out the Cleveland Indians and Chicago White Sox. The American League East was clinched by the New York Yankees on September 21. No great surprise there, as they were favored by many, given their prodigious hitting and pitching talent. But the Boston Red Sox and Tampa Bay Rays were still battling for a Wild Card spot, with the Red Sox in second place and the Rays in third in the powerful AL East. And the defending AL Champion Texas Rangers held off the Los Angeles Angels of Anaheim, strange name and all, taking the AL West on September 23.

Over in the National League, the Philadelphia Phillies rode a stellar pitching staff of reacquired Cliff Lee, Cy Young candidate Roy Halladay, Roy Oswalt, Cole Hamels, and rookie Vance Worley to a franchise-record 102 wins. On September 17, the Phillies won their fifth straight NL East title. The NL Central provided a little more excitement, with the upstart Milwaukee Brewers staying on in the second half to take the division on September 23. It was the Brewers' first division title in 29 years – and that was when they were in the American League! And over in the NL West, the Arizona Diamondbacks surprised many by going from last in 2010 to win the division by defeating the defending World Series Champion San Francisco Giants, also on September 23.

But the Wild Card teams were still undecided. Even those races looked fairly done as the season moved to its closing weeks. Let's pause here for a unique tutorial on this Wild Card business for those who have not mastered the arcane subtleties of its permutations, if anyone really has. (For those of you who are already down with this, skip ahead or go to YouTube and check out the 1954 World Series game with The Catch by Willie Mays. We'll get back to you in a moment.)

A Wild Card team is a backdoor interloper, if you will, a team that sneaks in. It's not that such teams are undeserving or untalented. In fact, they may have better records than division winners. Because the powers that be wanted more fan interest – and let's face it – more money, they allowed two more teams into the postseason party. These so-called Wild Card teams are ones that have not won their respective divisions, so they can get a second chance. They don't even have to have a winning record. Some purists loathe the whole deal, but those folks (I harbor some of these feelings myself, if you want to know the truth) would be happy with an alignment of just the American League and just the National League, no divisions at all. But we are never going back to that, so hush up. Baseball copied, or "borrowed," the wild card scheme from other sports in the United States that had had it for years. Going back to the late

Sixties and early Seventies, the National Basketball Association, the National Football League, and the National Hockey League all had some form of it. But baseball has always been more conservative about tampering with its traditions, and MLB resisted introducing wild card scenarios. Finally, players and owners agreed to inaugurate it for the 1994 postseason, except there wasn't a 1994 postseason. A strike by the players, and hardened stances from owners and players alike, ended the season prematurely. There were no playoffs and no World Series. So, 1995 turned out to be the inaugural year of the Wild Card (featuring the New York Yankees and Colorado Rockies as Wild Card playoff teams, if you must know).

Major League Rule 33 of the Major League Constitution covers the byzantine standards of the Wild Card. Since these regulations are so hard to find anywhere, and because Mr. Michael Teevan of the Office of the Commissioner was so generous to share them with us, let's take a closer look. The legalistic phrasing sounds a little like a document from the Vatican, or from the House of Lords. Look how the Wild Card is defined: "The Commissioner shall award a position in one Division Series in each Major League to the Club that won the highest percentage of its games during the championship season among the Clubs that were not Division champions. Such

Club shall be referred to as the Wild Card Club in its
League." Ahem. Adjust smoking jacket. Sip sherry. If
the Wild Card team is in the same division as the
team with the best record in the league, they can't
play each other. The Wild Card team has to face the
team with the second-best record. Also, the Wild
Card teams do not have home-field advantage in the
scheduling during the two rounds of playoffs before
the World Series.

What happens when there is a tie for the Wild Card
after 162 games are played? A one-game tiebreaker is
played, with home-field advantage determined by
head-to-head regular season record among the tied
teams. That has been the rule since the start of the
2009 season. Before that it was a coin flip, but
performance-based criteria were deemed more fair. If
at all possible, tiebreaker games are played on the first
day after the regular season. MLB has contingency
plans, especially for potential three-way tie scenarios,
but that has never happened. Yet. Nevertheless, there
are stipulations for bizarre, but certainly not
impossible, tiebreaker scenarios. For example, if two
clubs from the same division are tied but both are
assured of participating in the postseason, then the
first tiebreaker to determine which club is the division
champion and which club is the Wild Card would be
their season-series record. If two teams are tied for a
division title and the Wild Card is also shared with a

third team, here's what would happen. The two teams tied for the division lead would play the one-game tiebreaker, with the winner being declared the division champion. The losing team would then play the club from the other division for the Wild Card. If three – yikes! – clubs were tied for first place in the division with an identical winning percentage at the end of the regular season, then the tie would be broken by designating the clubs as A, B, and C, with those designations based on the clubs' records against each another. They would play tie-breaking games as follows: Club A would host Club B right after the regular season. The winner of the A vs. B game would then host Club C. The winner of the A/B vs. C game would be declared the division champion. Whew!

Starting in 2012, a play-in game is officially part of the mix. In effect, that institutionalizes a tiebreaker game. The new playoff format puts two more teams in each league into the postseason, albeit for as little as one game. And that means a starry-night Wild Card drama like September 28, 2011, will never happen again, at least not with the same scenarios in play.

To finish this Wild Card seminar, a few historical tidbits: the 2002 World Series featured the first Fall Classic of two Wild Card teams: the Anaheim Angels (when they were merely the Anaheim Angels) and the San Francisco Giants. (The Angels won, and broke my heart, another story for another time.) Other World Series won by Wild Card teams have included the Florida Marlins, twice (1997, 2003), the Boston Red Sox, famed of this story, in 2004, and the Saint Louis Cardinals, ultimate fighting heroes of this epic, in 2011.

So, back to our story. Who were the Wild Card candidates for 2011? For most of September, it seemed pretty simple. In the NL, it was almost certainly Atlanta, followed by an outside chance for Saint Louis, with an even slimmer chance for San Francisco. Earlier in the month, you could statistically include the Dodgers as well. In the AL, you had New York (which was more likely to take the AL East), Boston, and Tampa Bay, with a long, long shot of Anaheim of Los Angeles and even Toronto. But how realistic were the chances of these teams? Daily postings at Coolstandings.com went so far as to calculate the odds of a team making the playoffs. According to Coolstandings.com, which makes for fascinating reading in retrospect, on September 21 Boston enjoyed and 87.3% chance of making the playoffs, Los Angeles 8.8%, and Tampa Bay 4.5%. In the National League, on the same date, they estimated playoff prospects at 63.9% for Atlanta, 34.6% for St. Louis, and 2.2% for San Francisco. Go back a week earlier, to September 14, and Coolstandings figured a 93.2% playoff chance for Boston, 4.8% for Tampa Bay, and 13% for Los Angeles, and in the NL, 96.2% for Atlanta, 4.3% for St. Louis, and 0.7% for San Francisco. After the division titles were established, the clear favorites for Wild Card were still the Atlanta Braves in the National League and the Boston Red Sox in the American League. Clear favorites, but hardly certain. Only time — and fate — would tell.

Then the calendar turned to September. And the baseball gods and goddesses jiggled the celestial orbits of the sport's heavenly bodies. Things got a little crazy.

Chapter 3
Other Stellar Endings

"How ridiculous and how strange to be surprised at
anything which happens in life."

Marcus Aurelius, *Meditations*

Over the years, baseball has majored in the art of the
surprise. The sport has enjoyed many season-ending
dramatics, with Bobby Thomson's "The Shot Heard
'Round the World" in October 1951 arguably its most
notable. To give September 28, 2011, a broad
historical perspective, let's enter a time machine and
walk through a handfull of scintillating season
finishes.

Any baseball fan has heard it. "The Giants win the
pennant! The Giants win the pennant" shouted as a
manic litany by announcer Russ Hodges on October
3, 1951. It is cued up so often that it might easily
lapse into the category of sports or broadcasting cliché.

But it is unquestionably etched forever into the national consciousness. Bobby Thomson's game-ending ("walkoff" was not part of the lexicon) home run against the Brooklyn Dodgers remains forever an icon of dramatic sports victories. It is emblematic of the comeback, the shock, the collapse. Although tainted by later revelations of sign stealing, the game and the homer still stand as testaments to the high drama of American sports. Don DeLillo began his award-winning novel *Underground* with a fictionalized account of the game, later published separately as *Pafko at the Wall*. And the tragic side of the triumph coin has always borne the image of Dodger pitcher Ralph Branca. Unfortunately, even though he and Thomson, wedded by fate and history, became close friends, all his life Branca had to fight against the stereotype he had become. Such fixed views become cartoon depictions of the real thing. And in a memoir late in life, Branca sought to write his own epitaph, as it were, correcting the mistaken impression that many had held of his career.

The stellar ending of 1951 capped a long road back for the New York Giants. They were 13.5 games behind the Brooklyn Dodgers on August 11 and had climbed back to end in a tie on the last day of the season. The "Shot Heard Round the World" propelled the Giants into the postseason because they had just taken the second win of a special three-game playoff. This was a pure time in baseball. There were no divisional series, no championship series. Each league had eight teams and the pennant winners of each league proceeded straight to the World Series – unless – as was the case here – a special playoff were required.

Keep in mind that the Dodgers and Giants were rivals unlike any others before or since. They were two National League teams from the same city, different boroughs. At Brooklyn's Ebbets Field, the visiting and home clubhouses were near each other and in the pennant run of 1951 police had to separate the factions.

Bobby Thomson's home run in 1951 is mythic. After all, even the name it goes by, The Shot Heard Round the World, puts it in an American pantheon because that is the same phrase traditionally used to describe events on April 19, 1775, marking the start of the American Revolution, the Battle of Lexington and Concord. And further proof of the event becoming shrouded in myth and legend is the way it veers from reality to fantasy. Only 34,320 paying customers are recorded in the box score for that game (capacity was at 55,000 for the Polo Grounds, now a site of a housing project). It is likely that over the years more like 1,340,320 claimed they were at that game. Just as tens of thousands more than the 29,518 fans at

Tropicana Field in St. Petersburg and 45,350 at
Turner Field in Atlanta are likely to boast they were
there, when clearly they were not.

Baseball's memory vault is peculiar, unlike other
American sports. Today's fans put ultimate and total
importance on winning the World Series, the whole
enchilada, but many of its greatest moments enshrine
games that fell short of that goal. (Today many call
you a loser if you do not win it all.) But who
remembers that the New York Giants won the
pennant in 1951 but lost the World Series? (The
answer is wincingly easy: Yankees fans.) Carlton
Fisk's iconic home run in 1976 is the most
memorable moment from that Fall Classic, even
though the Cincinnati Reds won the Series, not the
Red Sox (back in the days when they were under the
Curse). In other words, baseball's collective scrapbook
of platinum memories is fickle, and it is hardly based
on winning or losing. As games like those of
September 28, 2011, fade into memory, the facts of
the game run the risk of becoming jumbled and
naturally selective recollections (was Marcel Proust a
closet, um, baseball fan?).

The basic game facts of October 3, 1951, now seem
nearly unremarkable: the contest lasted 2:28, the
winning pitcher was Larry Jansen, Ralph Branca, who
pitched to one batter was the hard-luck and unfairly

remembered loser, and the Giants won 5-4 with a four-run outburst in the bottom of the ninth inning after they trailed 4-1. Brooklyn had scored three in the top of the eighth, the game had eight hits apiece, no errors, and only one homer (that homer). Sounds pedestrian? Doesn't matter. Boom! One home run. An electric shock, the rally of a team given up for dead. A team that may have used up all its psychic energy and karma so much so that they were spent and drained, thereby losing the Series.

Why do we love it? Or hate it? Because of the sheer ludicrousness of it, the inexplicable foolishness of it, the same way the triple ka-ching of the slot machine pays off so much with flashing lights and sirens and the guys in the jackets have to escort you to the back room to tell you you just won $100,000. Or you just placed your life savings on one spin of the roulette wheel. And lost. Just like that.

•   •   •

Bobby Thomson's homer and its straight-to-the-World-Series result is legendary, to be sure, but an arguably close rival is The Bucky Dent Game of the New York Yankees at the Boston Red Sox, played October 2, 1978. If the Giants Win the Pennant! Giants Win the Pennant! Game is the ying, the Bucky Dent Home Run Game is the yang. This eponymous game is the American League version of the same amalgam of tragedy and triumph, desolation and elation that the 1951 contest incarnated. One side gets to rub salt in the wound of its opponent until some high priest exorcises the demons. From 1978 until 2004, Yankees fans could smugly torture Red Sox fans via this single game. And the Beantowners could summon no reply until 2004, when they came from 0-3 in a Championship Series to oust the Yankees and simultaneously cast out demons by ultimately ending the Curse of the Babe and win the World Series. (But etiquette would still caution against ever mentioning the Bucky Dent Home Run Game to a Red Sox devotee.)

Again, the statistical facts of the game recede in memory and pale in comparison to stilled moments of shock and awe. What are the facts? The Yankees, in a tumultuous season that saw manager Billy Martin fired and Bob Lemon hired, came from 14 games behind the Red Sox on July 19 to end the regular season in a tie. The Red Sox that year had faltered badly in the first part of September, losing 14 out of 17 games, but they won their final eight games and tied the Yankees, buoying the hopes of a region and setting the stage for high drama.

In a one-game tiebreaker at Fenway Park, Yankees shortstop Bucky Dent, a weak hitter with four homers and a .243 average on the season, stunned the home crowd by lofting a three-run homer off starter Mike Torrez. The shot that cleared the 37-foot Green Monster catapulted the Yankees to a 3-2 lead in the seventh inning. The Bronx Bombers would add another run in the seventh, extending their lead to 4-2 – this after the Red Sox had held a 2-0 edge through six innings. In the top of the eighth the Yankees made it 5-2, but when the Red Sox answered with two runs, closing the gap to 5-4, hope was resurrected for Red Sox Nation – for the 32,925 in the stands and legions elsewhere. As the prolific baseball author Harvey Frommer recounted the climax, as memorialized at Baseball-Almanac.com: "Dent fouled the second pitch off his foot. The count was one and one. There was a brief delay as the Yankees trainer tended to Dent. Mickey Rivers, the on-deck-batter, pointed out that there was a crack in the handsome infielder's bat. Dent borrowed a bat from Rivers. All set, Dent swung at the next pitch; the ball cleared the infield heading out to the left field wall. The wind and destiny moved the ball higher to its date with the Green Monster. 'Deep to left!' Bill White, Yankees broadcaster shouted, 'Yastrzemski will not get it!'"

Popular memory for many has the home run as a walkoff, but it was not. The Red Sox would threaten in the home half of the ninth, but future Hall of

Famer Carl Yastrzemski would weakly pop out to end the game and Bucky Dent would be forever a hero in Yankeeland and eternally scorned in New England and beyond.

Games like these are said to be life-changing, and it is not an exaggeration. My friend Dan Valenti and I worked together in 1978 on the copy desk at The (Syracuse) Post-Standard. He was and remains a fan of the Boston Red Sox. Until I wrote this book, I had held fast to a recollection that on the day of the Bucky Dent home run, my friend experienced, shall we say, a malaise that prevented him from fully realizing his capacities in the newsroom. Not having anticipated such malaise, Valenti failed to warn his employers of the diminution of his talents and skills. He was fired. But he told me a revised version of his firing after all these years. "The night before, I left a note saying I would be in to work after the game. The note was a joke. That's the part of the story no one ever knew or thought to ask me. [Editor] George Carr was a huge Yankees fan, and the note was my way of needling. I was feeling chippy." As it turned out, Valenti really couldn't make it into the newsroom at the appointed work time owing to car-repair problems. "Finally the garage calls. The car is ready. I speed walk and jog to pick it up and make the short drive to the paper. When I got into the newsroom, I could feel the tension. I figured it was from the ballgame, which was on the TV in the sports department. It was not. It was over little ol' me. I was fired."

Valenti continued, "I got home in time to watch Bucky Dent loft a pop fly into the Monster netting." Life changing? "It was perfect for my subsequent career. 'Way leads on to way,' as the famous Frost poem goes," he reflected. Dan Valenti has gone on to write 18 books, 11 on baseball — many on the Red Sox.

• • •

September 26 was the penultimate game of the 154-game season in 1959. The Milwaukee Braves defeated the Philadelphia Phillies 3-2, while the no-more-from-Brooklyn and now residing in Los Angeles Dodgers had fallen to the Chicago Cubs, 12-2. With one day of the season remaining, the Braves and Dodgers were tied for the NL lead (there were only eight teams in the league). On this same day, September 26 (check those astrological tables again, boys and girls) the San Francisco Giants beat the Saint Louis Cardinals, 4-0, check, in a rain-shortened affair, with Giants hurler Sam Jones spinning a seven-inning no-hitter! The next day, September 27, the Los Angeles Dodgers trounced the Cubs 7-1 and the Braves beat the Phils, 5-2, meaning the Dodgers and

Braves would meet in a best-of-three playoff. Sandy
Koufax met Lew Burdette in the first of the playoff
games, in Milwaukee. And Eddie Mathews passed
Ernie Banks for the home run title by virtue of his
performance in a playoff game in 1959. But get this:
the Giants had a chance for a tie! If both the Dodgers
and Braves lost, and the Giants had won both games
of their doubleheader, the Giants would have entered
into a three-way tie. God and the commish at the
time only know what would've happened in that event.

• • •

The term "playoffs" as it pertains to this era is
misleading if confused with today's use. A playoff
game was part of the regular season, an extension that
determined who would get to play in the only
postseason there was: the World Series. Twice before
in NL history were there playoffs of this sort: the
aforementioned 1951 and in 1946, when the Dodgers
succumbed to the Cardinals in two games. In the first
game, played in St. Louis on October 1, the Cards
beat Brooklyn 4-2, with Ralph Branca being the
losing pitcher. The Redbirds were led by catcher Joe
Garagiola (later a famous announcer and TV
personality), who went 3 for 4 with two runs batted in,
and pitcher H. Pollet, who pitched a complete game.
The Cardinals clinched the pennant by winning the

second playoff game, in Brooklyn two days later, 8-4, while pounding out 13 hits.

• • •

"DEWEY BEATS TRUMAN," the immortally wrong headline about the results of the 1948 presidential election, was not the only big surprise that year. In baseball, nearly every sports pundit had predicted that either the New York Yankees or the Boston Red Sox would win the American League pennant. Most AL managers, too, were of the same opinion. After a 7-0 win against Boston at the end of May, Yankees skipper Bucky Harris proclaimed that his team would take the pennant, even though they were in second place. Boston fans in particular were excited that year because they saw a realistic chance of an all-Boston World Series, since the Boston Braves were heavy favorites over in the National League. Despite the bold predictions and fervent hopes, the AL pennant chase was anything but a foregone conclusion. It was a thriller until the end. In the closing days of September, the Cleveland Indians, Boston Red Sox, and New York Yankees were tied, at 91-56. Seven games remained under the 154-game schedule of that era. With three games remaining, the Tribe led both the Yanks and the Sox by two games. As October began, Cleveland clung to a lead of one and a half games over both the Yankees and the Red

Sox, who would end the regular season with a two-game set against each other. After the Indians lost the first game of a three-game series finale to the Detroit Tigers, their lead shrunk to one game. Could the season end with three teams sharing identical records, something that had never happened? Well, it could. But on the season's next-to-last day, the Indians won while the Yankees lost, preserving the possibility of a two-way tie but nullifying the May boast of the Yankees' manager. As it turned out, the major league baseball season of 1948 did end in a tie – at 96-58 – because the Indians lost and the Red sox won on October 3. Therefore, on the next day, the American League held its first playoff game, at Boston's Fenway Park. (The two leagues differed at this time: the Nationals followed a best-of-three format, while the Americans went by a one-game tiebreaker to enter the Fall Classic.)

Why us, all the time? That's what the Red Sox faithful do have a right to ask. Just a passing glance at history's broad Boston baseball brush tells you why Red Sox fans might grasp at paranormal explanations for their fate over the years. You begin to see why they felt the Curse of the Bambino was on them, dooming them from the time their owner let Babe Ruth escape to the New York Yankees. As for the 1948 playoff game, Cleveland's starter was rookie sensation Gene Bearden, a knuckleballer who would

finish his debut season with a 20-7 record, a 2.43
ERA, and six shutouts. The Red Sox countered with
Denny Galehouse, a right hander and former Indian
who had thus far amassed an unimpressive 8-7 record,
and would finish with a 4.00 ERA and one shutout.
And therein perhaps lay the Red Sox' fatal error:
manager Joe McCarthy (yes, curse and conspiracy
theorists, the longtime Yankees manager) did not
start with Mel Parnell, who had a 15-8 record, 3.14
ERA and a shutout. Moreover, Parnell had already
beaten the Indians thrice before in the 1948 season.
According to Red Sox chroniclers Milton Cole and
Jim Kaplan, McCarthy claimed he had to go with
Galehouse because his was the only rested arm, an
assertion denied by Parnell and fellow pitcher Ellis
Kinder, a right hander who went to build a reputable
career as both a starter and reliever, foreshadowing
the path of Hall of Famer Dennis Eckersley. (Maybe
McCarthy was leery of Kinder's fortunes at Fenway,
since the previous year, on May 17, a seagull
reportedly delivered a smelt on Kinder during a game
while he was with the visiting Saint Louis Browns.
But he did win the game.)

As for the one-game playoff, it proved to be fairly
anti-climactic, at least in terms of competitiveness.
The Indians readily prevailed over the Bosox, 8-3, led
by Bearden's complete game, one-earned-run
performance. It allowed Cleveland into the Fall

Classic for the first time since 1920. They would not be there again until 1954, and the Red Sox would not get there until 1967. Cleveland third baseman Ken Keltner's hitting helped Bearden's cause by rapping a single, double, and three-run bomb. AL MVP and future Hall of Fame shortstop Lou Boudreau, who also just happened to be Cleveland's manager, added two homers of his own in the Indians' clinching victory, which ultimately led to a World Series victory. As of this writing, they have not had another one, the longest such drought in the American League. The Cubs' World Series drought leads the National League, and the Major Leagues, in terms of years without a World Series Championship.

• • •

Is this an exhaustive and definitive accounting of season-ending fireworks? Hardly. Indeed other years featured playoffs. The 1962 season saw a reprise of the Dodgers-Giants pennant playoffs, with the Giants giving the Dodgers a nightmarish case of deja vu on October 3, eleven years to the day of Bobby Thomson's shot. The Giants rallied for four runs in the ninth – again! – this time in Los Angeles, to defeat the Dodgers 6-4 in a game featuring seven errors. Talk about bad karma.

The Dodgers, whose penchant for late-season high drama and numbing defeat paralleled the similar frequent fate of the Boston Red Sox, were at it again in 1980. The Bums fashioned a three-game sweep, each by a margin of one run, of the first-place Houston Astros to end the season in a tie with the team formerly known as the Colt .45s. By this point, the National League had done away with the best-of-three tiebreaker playoff, going to a one-game tiebreaker (as the AL had always done) when divisional play began, in 1969. The 1980 NL West title went to the Astros, their first postseason entry, as Joe Niekro held off the Dodgers, 7-1, for his twentieth win. Art Howe, who would go on to manage the Astros, had a homer and four RBIs.

So baseball history is replete with ridiculous surprises, to paraphrase that famous DS (Designated Stoic) Marcus Aurelius. Take your pick from the surprise bin: the Mariners beating the Angels to win the AL West in 1995, the Cubs eliminating the Giants for the Wild Card in 1998, the Mets blanking the Reds for the Wild Card in 1999, or the surging Rockies beating the Padres for the Wild Card in 2007 (with three runs in the bottom of the ninth). How about the White Sox two-hitting the Twins to take the AL Central in 2008? Or the Twins taking the Tigers with a run in the ninth to win the AL Central crown in 2009?

We can even go back more than a hundred years to 1908, when the Giants and Cubs ended the season tied owing to what is typically described as "Merkle's Boner," a base-running gaffe (or was it?) by the Giants' young first baseman, Fred Merkle. Following a common practice of the day, he failed to touch second base on what would have been a game-ending play as the winning run scored. The Cubs appealed the play, fans streamed onto the Polo Grounds field, chaos ensued, and the game was called tied – and played over, days later. The Chicago Cubs won the makeup contest and proceeded to win the World Series. They have not won it again since 1908. Maybe capitalizing on Merkle's Boner cursed the Cubs.

Curses or not, it is time for us to release the pause button and click play. Players with names like David Freese, Evan Longoria, Craig Kimbrel, and Jonathan Papelbon are waiting in the wings (although Cookie Lavagetto might be my favorite baseball name of all time).

Chapter 4
The Road to September

"Every run like this is a life – a little life, I know – but
a life as full of misery and happiness and things
happening as you can ever get really around yourself."

Alan Sillitoe, *The Loneliness of the Long-Distance
Runner*

For the wild card scenarios described earlier to make
sense, fans need a sense of the upward, and
downward, trends of the four teams with so much at
stake. Quite simply, two things happened: Tampa
and St. Louis did extraordinarily well at precisely the
time Boston and Atlanta went flat.

But the Boston Red Sox and Tampa Bay Rays were
still battling for a Wild Card spot, with the Red Sox
in second place and the Rays in third in the powerful
AL East. And the defending AL Champion Texas
Rangers held off the Los Angeles Angels of Anaheim,

strange name and all, taking the AL West on
September 23.

The NL Central provided a little more excitement,
with the upstart Milwaukee Brewers staying on in the
second half to take the division on September 23. It
was the Brewers' first division title in 29 years – and
that was when they were in the American League!
And over in the NL West, the Arizona
Diamondbacks surprised many by going from last in
2010 to win the division by defeating the defending
World Series Champion San Francisco Giants, also
on September 23.

The Braves, who had won their first Wild Card slot
in 2010, were steady and strong in 2011, with the
team posting winning records for May (17-11), June
(17-9), July (16-11), and August (17-9). Managed by
first-year skipper Fredi Gonzalez, taking over for
legend Bobby Cox, the Braves, by the end of August,
were 80-55, seven and a half games behind the
Phillies but eight and a half games ahead of the Saint
Louis Cardinals in the Wild Card, with 27 games to
play. Not a given to win anything, but a good position
to be in. A modestly comfortable cushion, but not
without an annoying spring or two popping up from
the old couch. The Braves' success thus far was
propelled by their perennial strength, with a starting
rotation of veterans Tim Hudson and Derek Lowe,

followed by Jair Jurrjens, Brandon Beachy, Mike
Minor, and Tommy Hanson (who became disabled).
Their bullpen was led by Jonny Venters and
astonishing rookie Craig Kimbrel, who by August 31
had racked up a record 41 saves, eclipsing the record
set by Neftali Feliz of the Texas Rangers a year earlier.
Kimbrel also had a stingy 1.64 ERA on August 31.
Their hitting was more problematic, with slugger
Dan Uggla inconsistent, former rookie sensation
Jason Heyward struggling, and fan favorite Chipper
Jones respectable, but a shadow of his former self.
Rookie first baseman Freddie Freeman provided
some punch, with 18 homers and 64 RBIs thus far,
and a respectable .293 batting average.

As for the Boston Red Sox, their season's journey was
more enigmatic and zigzag. After missing the playoffs
in 2010, the Red Sox were determined to change that.
In the offseason they traded for Padres slugger Adrian
Gonzalez and signed free agent outfielder Carl
Crawford. To say that hopes were high might be an
understatement. Or, to put it another way, the
"irrational exuberance" (to use the famous phrase of
former Federal Reserve chairman Alan Greenspan) of
some observers was, well, irrational. (But that's how
fans are.) Back in the Hot Stove League days of
January 2011, Eric Ortiz at NESN went so far as to
predict that the 2011 Boston Red Sox "could unseat
the 1927 Yankees as the greatest major league team of

all time," also comparing the team that had yet to play a game to the 1976 Cincinnati Reds and the 1970 Orioles. As if to insult such passionate hope, reality intervened rudely in April. The Bosox started horribly. They lost their first six games and went 11-15 in April. Maybe they were experiencing the heretofore unknown T.S. Eliot Curse, because after all, he declared that "April is the cruellest month." But things really did get a lot better, with Boston, like Atlanta, having winning records in May (19-10), June (16-9), July (20-6), and August (17-12). Losing only six games in July, Red Sox pitchers dominated, with notable performances by newcomer Alfredo Aceves, who won four games in relief in the span, and John Lackey winning four starts and Josh Beckett three. Jonathan Papelbon recorded nine saves in the month. The Red Sox continued winning in August, though at a cooler pace. And on August 31, Boston finished the month by topping the archrival New York Yankees 9-5, leading Josh Beckett, now 12-5, to his fourth victory with no losses against the Yankees for the season thus far. He was helped by home runs from Jacoby Ellsbury (24th), David Ortiz (28th), and Jason Varitek (10th). As August ended, the Red Sox were a very respectable 83-52, one and a half games ahead of the Yankees atop the AL East. They rightfully had their eyes on the prize of the division title. Oh, the Wild Card? The Red Sox and Yankees shared a lead of seven and a half games over the

Tampa Bay Rays, with the Red Sox having 27 games
to play. Just like the Braves. A few dozen other teams
would have paid millions to be in that position.
(Actually, they all paid millions to be in that
position.)

And what about Joe Maddon and his Tampa Bay
Rays? It turns out that they too were afflicted with
the T.S. Eliot Curse, starting April off by losing their
first six games. The difference with Tampa Bay was
that they were not predicted to be the 1927 Yankees
redux. In the first week of April 2011, they would no
doubt have been pleased, or at least felt respected, if
they had been predicted to be the reincarnation of the
2008 Tampa Bay Rays. That team went to the Fall
Classic but fell four games to one, to the Philadelphia
Phillies. That team had also been the team with a
new name, the Rays, instead of the previously dubbed
Devil Rays. Maybe the 2011 Rays should have been
renamed the Goners because gone were relief pitchers
Dan Wheeler (to Boston, see above), Randy Choate
(to the Marlins), closer Rafael Soriano (to the
Yankees), and starting pitcher Matt Garza (to the
Cubs). And gone was longtime star outfielder Carl
Crawford (7 years, $124 million, to the Red Sox,
again, see above). Gone also were first baseman
Carlos Pena (to the Cubs? what was it with the Rays
and the Cubs that winter?) and shortstop Jason
Bartlett (to the Padres). Nevertheless, the Rays

managed to "uncruel" April, even with third baseman
Evan Longoria injured with a strained obligue. They
finished the month with 15 wins and 12 losses,
becoming the first team in American League history
to start the season with six straight losses only to
salvage a winning April. (Hey, baseball has a "record"
for nearly everything.) The team followed with a
winning May, barely (14-13) and June (16-11) and a
losing July (11-15). (You might say the Rays' monthly
records were inconstant, which gives us an excuse for
a brief Shakespearean interlude: "O, swear not by the
moon, the fickle moon, the inconstant moon, that
monthly changes in her circle orb." Baseball has
always appealed to thinkers and poets, as well as to
Tinkers to Evers to Chance. But we digress.) Perhaps
the Rays' losing record in July was due in part to
fatigue. They lost a 16-inning game to the Red Sox,
1-0, a contest that began on July 17 and ended five
hours and 42 minutes later, at 1:35 a.m. With an 18-
10 August, the retooled Rays, featuring All-Star
pitchers David Price and James Shields and outfielder
Matt Joyce, stood at 74-61, in third place in the
American League East, nine games behind the
Yankees and seven and a half games behind in the
Wild Card race. They were a long shot, but
undaunted.

The last member of this ensemble cast of characters
(dramatis personae, for our newly won Shakespearean

fans) is the Saint Louis Cardinals. Coming off a non-playoff year, they entered 2011 without major differences in personnel but lots of looming question marks, chief among them the status of superstar first baseman Albert Pujols, who would become a free agent after the season, and Tony LaRussa, managing in what could become his last year under contract. Newcomers included Lance Berkman in the outfield, Jake Westbrook on the mound, and Nick Punto in the infield. The season's first game, against the Padres, was inauspicious. Closer Ryan Franklin gave up a ninth-inning game-tying homer, the Cardinals lost in 11 innings, and outfielder Matt Holliday had an emergency appendectomy the day after the game. They went 16-11 in April, holding a first-place lead over the Milwaukee Brewers by two games and went 17-12 in May. Major injuries beset the team. Third baseman David Freese broke a bone in his hand in May, Punto joined him on the DL in May, and Pujols sustained a wrist injury in June, when the Redbirds went 11-15, which included a stretch of 3-12. A feckless Franklin was released in June. In July, the Cards went 13-13, but more notably Pujols returned to the lineup, much sooner than anticipated, and the team made major trades. From the Toronto Blue Jays, they got starter Edwin Jackson, relievers Marc Rzepczynski and Octavio Dotel, and outfielder Corey Patterson. From the Los Angeles Dodgers, Saint Louis got veteran shortstop Rafael Furcal.

Reaching a season low point, on August 24, the Cardinals were ten and a half games behind the Milwaukee Brewers in the NL Central and the same distance, in third place, in the Wild Card race, behind the Atlanta Braves. Although they recovered somewhat to end August (15-13), their eight and a half games behind the Brewers and the Braves hardly had them looking like playoff contenders.

So the pennant stew of September 2011 was simmering. Its ingredients contained no surprises, nothing shocking to the palate, no nouvelle cuisine oddities. But in the middle of several nights late in September a few anonymous chefs sneaked into the kitchen and silently tossed in some ingredients not called for in the standard recipe for pennant stews. Some of those spices they spinkled in have yet to be identified or named.

Chapter 5
"Happy Flight! Happy Flight!"

"The world is all gates, all opportunities, strings of
tension waiting to be struck."

Ralph Waldo Emerson

Baseball is an iron coil. Its spring tightens, sometimes
molasses-slowly, storing kinetic tension, waiting to
release it at mystically appointed moments. When the
coil is tight and seemingly secure, fans at the ballpark
chat about family, office gossip, politics, or games
from bygone days. Fans at home watching on TV run
to the bathroom or grab a beverage or snack.
Baseball's Victorian side allows for this, the fine art of
conversation in the midst of a crowd, or even a
moment of diversion or solitude. It allows for this
during moments of reprieve, when a contest is not
tight or when there is a lull. Granted, loudspeakers
blaring pop music or prompts from the stadium
organist make any conversation a challenge. The

distraction of HD animations and assorted other non-baseball shenanigans add to the conversational hurdles. And any in-game conversation may not even be with the person sitting next to you enjoying a micro-brewed beverage or an $8 coffee. These days, fans shamelessly make calls on cellphones while sitting in what Bill Lee has compared to a church, that is, a baseball stadium. Or thumbs are busy texting someone in Section 347 or in Minot, North Dakota, or checking Facebook. If we are lucky, though, fans might even be giving the rest of us in the real world live updates via Twitter, 140-character snippets from the scene. Readers will see those archived Tweets sprinkled throughout this narrative, placing specks of time in amber, preserved by Topsy.com and other services, for us to enjoy into digital eternity. You will also see occasional references or citations from various fan blogs (does anyone remember the term web log, its origin?). The community of Cardinals fans robustly embraces blogging. They seem to go a step further, with the team's front office engaging the e-community and coordinating events. This legion of fans is a new breed, not constrained by time zone or state borders. And these new fan configurations are engendering new loyalties and new bonds — even new intimacies — that previous generations of fans could not enjoy.

• • •

With the first pitch thrown by the Astros' Brett
Myers to the Cardinals' Jon Jay in Houston at 8:06
p.m. ET of September 28, all four Wild Card
contender games were now in progress. (If you really
must know, it was a four-seam baseball clocked at 88
miles per hour for a called strike.) No MLB Network
or ESPN Baseball Tonight viewer or remote Internet
follower had a realistic inkling of the drama to unfold,
unless the fan were a monastic clairvoyant living in
the eastern Himalayas. The tension infusing the
Cardinals at Astros game was both direct and indirect,
related to the game at hand as well as to other games,
other possibilities. If the Cardinals were to lose to the
Astros and the Atlanta Braves were to win, the
Cardinals would be packing their bags for
Destination Winter. And if both the Braves and
Cardinals were to win, or even if both were to lose,
the two would play a tiebreaker in St. Louis. So, even
if St. Louis did all it could to support its own chances
for the Wild Card in 2011, they still had no
guarantee of traversing the postseason portals. They
needed help from the Phillies, back in Atlanta some
554 miles away. By definition, even if the Cards-
Astros contest were a close one, it would not by itself
determine the Cardinals' Wild Card status.

As the Cardinals took the field, did they feel the hum
of the electromagnetic-cosmic force field of the
Phillies-Braves game, which had begun about an hour

earlier? Not by any reports that have surfaced. Scoreboard watching still involves old-fashioned linear skills like, well, actually looking at neon lights on stadium scoreboards (and the occasional surreptitious Tweet now and then). And minutes before the Cardinals went to bat, at 8:03 Dan Uggla slugged his thirty-sixth home run of the year, to put the Braves ahead, 3-1, in the third inning. In case the Cardinals or their legions of fans in Houston were mildly curious about rumblings in the American League, the scoreboard would note that a homer by the Orioles J.J. Hardy at 8:06 put the Red Sox in the hole 2-1, also in the third inning. Meanwhile, at 7:54, the Yankees' Mark Teixeira had connected for a grand slam, giving the New York Yankees a cozy 5-0 lead over the do-or-die Tampa Bay Rays in the top of their second inning.

Andy Levy @andylevy
MLB should just cancel the postseason. Not gonna top tonight.

The Cardinals' in their season finale faced the not-very-good Houstonians, a team that had unloaded its three best offensive players during the season. The star-crossed teams entered the evening with the Cards at 89-72 and the Astros at 56-105, poised to set a team record for losses. Game 162 would be the Astros' last under the Drayton McLane ownership group.

The Cardinals Fox (FSMW) broadcast noted that on this day in baseball history Rogers Hornsby finished with a .424 batting average in 1924, and Ted Williams went six for eight in a doubleheader to end the season at .406 in 1941.

The visitors' starting lineup, penned by Hall of Fame-bound manager Tony LaRussa, featured Jon Jay CF, Allen Craig LF, Albert Pujols 1B, former Astro Lance Berkman RF, David Freese 3B, Yadier Molina C, Skip Schumaker 2B, Nick Punto SS, and ace Chris Carpenter, coming in with a 10-9 mark. This would be the last starting lineup for a regular season game that LaRussa would devise. The guys wearing home jerseys, managed by Brad Mills, had a starting lineup of J.B. Shuck CF, Jose Altuve 2B, J.D. Martinez LF, Carlos Lee 1B, Brian Bogusevic RF, Jimmy Paredes 3B, Clint Barmes SS, Humberto Quintero C, and Brett Myers, 7-13 up to this point. Myers, from Jacksonville, Florida, stood at 6'4" and 240 pounds. With size like that, the guy could be a boxer, right? He was indeed an amateur boxer, and his father had trained Boxing Hall of Famers Larry Holmes and Michael Spinks. The thirty-one-year-old right hander had spent 2002-09 with the Philadelphia

Phillies, winning a World Series championship with them in 2008. Signed by Houston as a free agent, Myers was stellar his first year with them, in 2010, going 14-8 with a 3.14 ERA and his typical 200+ innings (223.2). He finished 2011 with a disappointing 7-14, 4.46 ERA, but he had surged in September, going 4-0 with a 1.24 ERA in his previous five starts. Furthermore, he had not permitted more than nine hits in any start since August 6. Carpenter, from Exeter, New Hampshire, 6'6", 230 pounds, was a pitcher who went 49-50 for the Toronto Blue Jays (1997-2002) before becoming one of the game's elite hurlers, going 95-42, with a slim 3.06 ERA for the Cardinals from 2004-11. Carpenter had struggled at Minute Maid Park, going 0-3 with an unsavory 4.62 ERA in his last five starts there. Worse yet, Carpenter had not won a start in Houston since 2005. However, to balance off that ominous statistic, he had good numbers for September in his career, going 21-10.

That tight spring of tension? It can sproing loose at any moment, even at the start of a game. And SPROING [capital letters, boldface italic] it did for Saint Louis. The Cardinals paraded 10 batters to the plate in the first inning. Successive singles by Jon Jay, Allen Craig, Albert Pujols, and Lance Berkman (doesn't he remind you of country singer Vince Gill?) tallied two runs before one out was recorded. A David

Freese double, a Skip Schumaker infield hit off Myers's glove, and a Nick Punto single at 8:23 p.m. made it 5-0, and it could have been worse for the Astros (Chris Carpenter struck out on a foul bunt; imagine if he had singled.). It was the most productive first inning of the Cardinals' season. Talk about timing. In the midst of this spree, Myers displayed a degree of irritation, eliciting a mound visit from manager Brad Mills.

It's not as if Myers saw the game as a throwaway. "I really wanted to win," he said. "I really wanted to go out there and put them out. It didn't work out." No, it didn't work out for Myers. With five hits yielded in his first 22 pitches, he buoyed the Cardinals and dug himself a deep hole. The more appropriate metaphor would be pugilistic: he was on the ropes. But he stayed in the game and settled down and battled.

Carpenter, the 2005 NL Cy Young, three-time All Star, and 2009 comeback Player of the Year, was all-business right from the start, striking out five of the first nine batters he faced. Carpenter was certainly mentally poised. "Going into that last day of the year, you try to eliminate the distractions," he was quoted as saying. "The games are obviously big games with consequences, but if you can simplify them and just concern yourself with executing your game plan, the easier it is." Carpenter could take further solace in the presence of his pitching coach, Dave Duncan, at a game for the first time since August 19, as his wife battled brain cancer.

Derrick Goold @dgoold
Cardinals now have a base hit from every spot in the lineup. They're not even through the third inning. #stlcards #Cardinals #braves

---

The game had allurements other than the Wild Card potential for the Saint Louis Cardinals. Albert Pujols came in with 98 RBIs, and he was aiming for 100. (He would fall one RBI short.) Pujols was also gunning for his eleventh straight year batting .300 or more. He came in at .300, and would also miss that mark, ending at .299. On top of all that, spectators did not know if it would be the last regular-season game for Pujols as a Cardinal, eliciting lots of camera flashes and applause for each Pujols at bat. (It was indeed his last regular-season game as a Cardinal; he signed as a free agent with the Angels.)

Things calmed down a bit after the first. Carpenter helped his cause with an RBI single in the third. In the fifth, Skip Schumaker scored David Freese, who had rapped his second double of the evening, making it a 7-0 lead. (Hold that thought: over in St. Pete, at

8:52 p.m. the Yankees also held a 7-0 lead over Tampa Bay. Not looking like a very exciting night, yet.) To be more accurate, I should add that things were never un-calm for the Astros hitters. Neither their bats nor their walking shoes ever came alive. Carpenter kept the Houston hitters sleepwalking into the Texas night, allowing one single in the fourth and another in the sixth. Myers trudged through five innings, yielding to reliever Wilton Lopez in the sixth, and showing a line of 10 hits, seven runs, six earned, with only one walk and three strikeouts.

Although this game looked easy, things were not very loosey-goosey for the Cards a mere thirty-five days earlier. As St. Louis Post-Dispatch columnist Joe Strauss reported, the slumping team held a Busch Stadium clubhouse meeting that seemed to turn their fortunes. "It was about not embarrassing ourselves," said Carpenter of the players' pow-wow. "It was about 'Let's go out and play hard. Stop pushing so hard. Let's go play and let our talent come out.'" "We felt like we played more relaxed this month than in any other month," Schumaker said. "We're having fun."

Reports from Cardinals fans who were at Minute Maid Park said it was almost like a home game. Large numbers of red-wearing St. Louis fans were in the house, knowing what was at stake and ready to celebrate. There is no current or former bitter rivalry

between the Astros and Cardinals. They did meet in
the 2004 and 2005 postseasons, with the Astros
advancing to the World Series in 2005, but there is
no deep animosity as there is, say, between the Cubs
and Cardinals. And in 2011 the Astros were one of
baseball's least successful teams, so they did not pose a
serious threat to the Cardinals (although weak teams
do have a penchant for doing just that). According to
local resident Tony Bender, a Cards fan who was at
the game, "The crowd all series was split 50-50
between Astros and Cardinals fans. Usually, you'll see
a large number of St. Louis fans during a regular
season series anyway, but at those last three games I
saw more than I ever had. I would believe that St.
Louis fans outnumbered Houston fans at Game 162
if you told me that it was a fact. By the end of the
game, Cardinals fans definitely did outnumber
everyone else."

Although Cardinals fans knew the import of this
game, they understood the early lead, coupled with
Carpenter's dominance, took the wind out of the sails
with respect to drama. In fact, at one point Rick
Horton and Al Hrabosky said during the
FoxSportsMidwest telecast, "It was supposed to be a
little more dramatic." Not that they minded.
(Viewing a game after the fact on MLB.tv has
advantages and disadvantages. For this fan, it is
entertaining and instructive to catch some of the

regional and local color. Promos for things like "Paintball Predator Hunt" just don't show up on national broadcasts. On the other hand, for some reason, perhaps related to rights and licensing, the archived video streaming blanks out studio updates. In this case, the updates were obviously related to the other games in progress, but after the announcers' lead-in, the audio goes silent. Maybe only "Premium" subscribers get to hear those studio updates.)

Meanwhile, two big games were going on in the National League, one here in Houston and the other in Atlanta. It is nearly impossible to convey the simultaneity. Physics (and metaphysics) makes it impossible to have been in Houston and Atlanta at the same time, but TV and the Internet make it almost possible, St. Thomas Aquinas, Plato, Albert Einstein, and Stephen Hawking to the contrary notwithstanding.

Etymological Dictionary Definition: *meanwhile*

mid-14c., from mean "middle, intermediate" + O.E. hwile, acc. of hwil "a space of time," from P.Gmc. *khwilo (cf. O.S. hwil, O.Fris. hwile, O.H.G. hwila, Ger. Weile, Goth. hveila "space of time, while"), originally "rest" (cf. O.N. hvila "bed," hvild "rest"), from PIE *qwi- "rest" (cf. Avestan shaitish "joy," O.Pers. šiyatish "joy," L. quies "rest, repose, quiet," O.C.S. po-koji "rest"). Notion of "period of rest" became in Germanic "period of time." Now largely superseded by time except in formulaic constructions (e.g. all the while). M.E. sense of "time spent in doing something" now only preserved in worthwhile and phrases such as worth (one's) while. As a conjunction (late O.E.), it represents O.E. þa hwile þe; form whiles is recorded from early 13c.; whilst is from late 14c., with excrescent -st as in amongst, amidst (see amid).

Kocak Translation: So that means, in medias res, in the middle of a space of time, in the midst of intermediate rest or repose or even joy, O ye ancient Frisians, Germans, Persians, Norsemen, and Olde English folk, the long wicks of a thousand firecrackers were sparkling from Houston to Atlanta, from Baltimore to St. Pete.

Karl Ravech @karlravechespn
Single most memorable night of baseball in my 18 years as host of baseball tonight... congrats rays and cardinals. Message is never give up

---

The Cardinals of the night of September 28 were not the Cardinals of April, May, or June. General Manager John Mozeliak had traded several players as the July 31 trading deadline loomed, obtaining starter Edwin Jackson, relievers Marc Rzepczynski and Octavio Dotel, shortstop Rafael Furcal and outfielder Corey Patterson. They also signed veteran lefty reliever Arthur Rhodes as a free agent. The moves seemed to be another factor in loosening the clubhouse. "I don't think anybody outside of our clubhouse gave us a chance then," recalled Nick Punto. "To be honest, there were probably people in our clubhouse who didn't give us much of a chance. But we never quit on ourselves." Furcal led a lightness and enthusiasm encapsulated in the cheer that had become a mantra in the season's closing days: "Happy flight! Happy flight!" As a cheer and a tonic, the chant roused the team as series ended and served as a reminder on this Houston trip of the happy ending that could await the team.

Is it bad I am not even paying attention to the crads [sic] game
VolsnCards via VivaElBirdos.com.

The Cardinals' players, coaches, and fans were clearly pleased with their team's performance, but obviously more scoreboard watching was in order.

We have a situation in Atlanta.
Pegasus via VivaElBirdos.com.

We lead HOU 0-8, NYY leads TB 7-0
BOX up 3-2, ATL up 3-2

bizarro land
d-dee via VivaElBirdos.com.

Please don't make me use my tickets for tomorrow
zach3315 via VivaElBirdos.com.

So as the Astros batters faced Chris Carpenter in the
bottom of the seventh inning, the Cardinals fans at
Minute Maid Park, attendance announced as 24,358,
cheered when they saw from the left-field scoreboard
that the Phillies and Braves were now tied at 3 at 9:56.
Carpenter noticed the joyful noise from the Cardinals'
fans and he permitted himself one guilty pleasure, one
pause from his workmanlike gem, and he checked out
the scoreboard. After the seventh, when Duncan
asked Carpenter how he felt, the answer was a
headline-in-the-making: "Fabulous."

Carpenter is pitching one of his best in a long time.
Where usual Carp pitches a gem and the offense
refuses to back him up... Now Carp is pitching a gem
with the offense backing him up, and every Cards fan
is watching the Braves. Poor Carp.
JStymie via VivaElBirdos.com.

Just for good measure, outfielder Allen Craig launched a home run in the ninth, his eleventh of the year and second in as many nights, to make it 8-0 at 10:18, which would be the final score. At 10:26 p.m., Carpenter retired the Astros' J.D. Martinez on a feeble grounder, the Cardinals rejoiced on the field in a joyful but businesslike manner, as befitted their sense of mission. The first turn of the screw was complete.

This has to be the mis exciting [sic] day in baseball in a long time
Paulspike via VivaElBirdos.com.

!!!!!!!!
I love baseball today.
clank via VivaElBirdos.com.

Carp
a man among boys today
huja via VivaElBirdos.com.

Notching his fifteenth career shutout at the most opportune time, the righthander was brilliant, fanning 11 while allowing only two hits and a walk in a tidy 106-pitch, two-hour twenty-minute endeavor, giving him an 11-9 record for the season. The Astros managed to get only one runner to second base; no one reached third. It was Carpenter's fourth complete game and second shutout of the season.

Tom Orf @mu4124
Carpenter 14th 10-strikeout game for the Cardinals, now 2nd only to Bob Gibson (74)

pourmecoffee @pourmecoffee
Everything is going to climax together at the exact same time, like in porn. #mlb

---

Pujols and Berkman hugged. Tony LaRussa took pictures with his cellphone, and then the team waited and watched. Yes, the St. Louis faithful lived out a measure of "watchful waiting," the sometimes agonizing procedure that doctors urge on patients. In this instance, the waiting was of the similarly powerless sort, watching events unfold in Atlanta.

"We were all sitting around in the clubhouse and training room," Cards GM John Mozeliak recalled, "watching every pitch and agonizing throughout those final moments."

And at 11:40 p.m. back East, when the Phillies' David Herndon extinguished the last embers of hope for the Braves, the Cardinals' long climb from 10 games behind in late August was done.

Dathan @dathan7
If there's ever, EVER been a more exciting day of baseball, in all of it's history, I'd love to hear abou tit! #MLB

"Most of us were in the food room [at Minute Maid Park]," Carpenter said. "All I can remember is the excitement in the room, the uproar in the clubhouse after that final out."

The jubilant Cards could now chant "Happy flight! Happy flight!" with full abandon, doused in Champagne.

Dan Shulman @dshulman_espn
For years to come, when teams are seemingly way out of it, we'll all be recalling the #rays and #cardinals comebacks of 2011. #neversaydie

---

Chapter 6
Waiting for Take-off

"Some things are destined to be – it just takes us a
couple of tries to get there."

J.R. Ward, *Lover Mine*

When it comes to dramatic impact, the stalwart and
knowledgeable fans of the St. Louis Cardinals are at
an emotional disadvantage in our narrative. Jumping
out to a five-run lead, the Redbirds lowered the
temperature of the four-game stew that was
simmering. Nevertheless, the fans I talked to
demonstrated deep respect for the game of baseball
and almost without exception displayed a keen
excitement for Baseball's Starry Night that went far
beyond the fortunes of their beloved team.

Dathan Brooks, 35, also known on Twitter as
@Dathan7, lives in suburban St. Louis, on the Illinois
side, about 25 minutes from his kitchen to Busch

Stadium. He works for a surgical instruments manufacturer and for recreation his life tends toward following the Cardinals. Back in 2000, he and five friends in a barbershop sextet sang the National Anthem on Fourth of July weekend at Busch Stadium, the old one. To do so, Dathan had to sell at least 500 tickets to the game and send an audition tape. He was inspired to do this via a dream the preceding Christmas. The dream, such as the kind you would imagine in a book of the Bible (from whence his name comes, from Numbers, but that's another story), instructed him that he and his cohort would be singing the National Anthem at a Cards game. The singing event, in turn, enabled Brooks to attend his first postseason games that year, allowing him to witness firsthand Rick Ankiel's famous wild-pitch meltdown (Ankiel since became an outfielder with slugging potential, electing for the Babe Ruth career path).

Although Dathan Brooks did not attend the Cardinals' finale in Houston (he has a daughter there), he recalls, "Lots of Cards fans were there. It was like a home game. By the fifth or sixth inning, you could hear the cheers for Carpenter just like it was at Busch Stadium."

Dathan oversees two blogs, TiedforFirst, which focuses on the Cardinals, and

GoodMorningGoodAfternoonGoodNight, plus he
contributes every Friday to the popular
i70baseball.com Cardinals blog.

On September 28, 2011, while the Redbirds were
playing in Houston, Dathan Brooks was in his living
room, at first merely watching the Cardinals' cozy
contest. "First and foremost, I'm a fan of baseball,
then I'm a Cardinals fan, then a fan of individual
players. And when things started happening, like the
Rays catching up against the Yankees and the close
games of the Braves-Phillies and Red Sox-Orioles, I
knew this was going to be a very rich night. I started
texting my brother in another time zone, in
Gainesville, Florida, saying, 'oh, wow, are you
watching this?'"

At one point, Dathan found he simply could not get
the Red Sox-Orioles game from his cable provider, so
he used his MLB.tv subscription on his laptop and
went from his TV to his laptop to his phone to text to
his television, switching channels. Plus, throw in a
little blogging and Tweeting for good measure. This
was, by his own admission, easier during the rain
delay in Baltimore.

"The best thing was that while this was all happening,
during the moment, I fully realized this could be the

greatest night in the history of baseball. Not afterward. I knew it then. It's a great feeling."

Dathan and I had an animated phone conversation, replete with interruptions and punctuated asides, reminiscing about that night and other baseball memories. I asked him if he was able to sleep after all the games for the Wild Card were played. "It's funny you say that. My friend Aaron called me around 1:15 a.m. because he just knew I'd be up. And he was right. And it turns out I probably didn't get to sleep until 3 or so, I was so amped up."

As a postscript, Brooks related how he had called company colleagues in or near all the participating cities, asking for the next day's newspapers or other memorabilia, to put in a shadow box or some other display. He belatedly discovered that one friend had been at the Trop but left in the seventh inning! "It goes to show you: never leave a game. You just don't know what might happen." That friend, though, did send newspapers and a Game 162 ticket stub. Of course, the best coda to all this for Cardinals' fans was winning the World Series, which the events of September 28 allowed the Cardinals admission to. And for Dathan Brooks, that culminated in attending the Game 7 clincher in St. Louis. Who knew this night would lead to that?

Christine Coleman (@ccoleman802) lives in Moline, Illinois, one of the Quad Cities in western Illinois-eastern Iowa along the Mississippi River. Moline is home to the Cardinals Class A minor league team. The Quad Cities River Bandits play in a handsome riverside ballpark in Davenport, Iowa. Born and raised in the Quad Cities area, she shares a birth date with Tim Wakefield, MLB's oldest player during the 2011 season. As she puts it on her Twitter profile, Christine is a marketing manager by day, and a writer before and after. And she's a Cardinals baseball fan all the time and senior Cardinals reporter for Aaron Miles' Fastball, a blog at Aerys Sports (Aaronmilesfastball.com). For those of you wondering, Aaron Miles was a journeyman infielder who toiled from 1995-2011 for five teams, twice with the Cardinals, 2006-08 and 2010. The "fastball" in the blog's title is a wry reference to former Cardinals' manager Tony LaRussa's penchant for using Miles for mop-up during blowouts. He had mixed success in this "short reliever" role (baseball-reference.com lists him at 5'8"), but his fastball did result in a handful of strikeouts.

"I actually wasn't nervous. I felt confident with Chris Carpenter pitching, and there wasn't drama at all to the Cardinals winning this. So when they got a big lead quickly, I knew that at the very worst, they'd play a tiebreaker game the next night. And, despite the fact Chris Carpenter is my favorite Cardinal, I switched over to watch the Phillies-Braves in the seventh inning – that outcome was not assured so it was more important! (Besides, I was DVR-ing the game so I knew I could watch it later.)"

Coleman watched the Cardinals' Game 162 on TV but also had her laptop handy, to share her emotions on Twitter and at her blog. Like her fellow Cards fans, she kept tabs on the St. Louis-Houston game as well as the Phillies-Atlanta game a time zone away. "I don't know that many Cards fans were even watching our game toward the end. I've always liked the Phillies, so rooting for them was fine."

Once the Cardinals easy triumph over the Astros was over, Christine switched to Fox Sports Midwest showing the Cardinals sitting in the locker room in Houston watching the Phillies and Braves too. "It was just so thrilling when Hunter Pence gave the Phillies the lead, and then they won – just so cool to see the Cardinals' joy in the locker room. I have a picture in my blog of Chris Carpenter and Albert Pujols hugging. That picture is from my TV!

"My friend Kelly called me right after the celebration was winding down – she lives in the Quad Cities also, but we met on Twitter and communicate that way most often. But she just wanted to talk, since it was

such an exciting night. This was before the two AL
games ended, so we didn't yet know how thrilling it
was going to be overall. We were talking and
watching what was still being shown of the Cardinals'
clubhouse, then both flipped to watch those other
two games. I cannot stand the Red Sox, going back to
the 2004 World Series, so I was beyond thrilled to see
the Orioles with the walk-off win. Then, of course,
minutes later, Evan Longoria hit that HR. I just
remember both Kelly and I screaming over the phone.
I'd kept tabs on both of those AL games early on but
then got caught up in my game and the Braves game
so had kind of lost track of how the Rays even came
back to tie it. But the endings of those two AL games
were just so amazing it seemed surreal – especially
with them ending basically back-to-back."

The Cardinals consume Coleman's attention daily.
Once the regular season arrives, her routine includes
watching every game while on Twitter with her
Twitterati community, which has been her modus
operandi since early in the 2009 season. For the last
10 or more years, she has been regularly conversant
about the Cardinals with her uncle, his brother-in-
law, and a friend via email. She typically attends a
couple of Cardinals games a year, either in St. Louis
or Chicago or Milwaukee.

"Where I live is more Cubs country than Cardinals, so at work there is only one serious Cardinals fan, but we start each day chatting about the previous day's activities. Much of the time, we enjoy talking with the many Cubs fans in the office. (We especially enjoyed it last October!) My family is similarly 'divided' – my uncle and I are the biggest Cardinals fans, with my 10-year-old nephew and niece also joining us as Cardinals fans. Everyone else in our extended family is a Cubs fan. So, family gatherings are entertaining, but it's all good- natured."

Christine shared some scrapbook recollections of baseball. "I have been a baseball fan for a very, very long time. My Grandpa used to play catch with me frequently when I was a kid, and I remember him taking one of my brothers and me to see our local minor league team (they were the Quad Cities Angels back then). Bob Feller was at one game and we got his autograph. I was maybe 10 and had no clue who Feller was. Although my Grandpa was very excited about Feller being there and told me about him, I didn't retain any of it unfortunately (and my Grandpa died when I was in high school). My Dad was my brother's baseball coach for five years, from ages 8 to 12, and our summers revolved around baseball."

One memory in particular echoes Doris Kearns Goodwin's father-daughter bond recounted in *Wait*

Till Next Year: "My Dad taught me how to keep score. I kept the scorebook for the team for a while. The Little League ballpark was a block away from our house, so I was always there even on the days my brother didn't play."

I have been impressed with the intricate and indelible detail that baseball fans associate with first games or other introductions to Major League baseball. Their earliest memories take on almost mythic proportions, with the precise and ceremonial retelling, say, of ancient stories of healing or redemption. Sure, that is heavy-handed and a stretch, but listen to earnest fans. Their stories are replete with vivid portraits or sound collages. Their retellings sometimes border on the evangelistic.

Coleman notes, "It wasn't until 1983 that I became an MLB fan. That was when we first got cable TV, so I was able to watch the Cubs on WGN. They became my team. My first real MLB memory is from that summer, from a game where the Cubs were playing the Cardinals. My family was at my Grandma's house. The Cubs had the bases loaded and Jody Davis was coming up. My brother said he'd give everyone $5 if he hit a homer. And he did! Though I never got the $5, I did realize just how cute Jody Davis was. So I continued to follow and love the Cubs, especially with the excitement of the 1984 season. In college, I even pursued an internship with the team's media relations office – which, through luck, I was hired for, January to June 1988. While it had some good points, obviously, it also was an eye-opening experience too.

"Once the 1988 season ended, I gave up following baseball for 10 years ... until Harry Caray died. (I'd talked with him regularly during my internship and he seemed almost like another grandpa to me.) I started following the Cubs again in 1998, which of course included the home run race between Sammy Sosa and Mark McGwire. And I really grew to like McGwire as that summer went on and the race heated up. So much that when the Cubs became the Cubs again in 1999 after their exciting 1998, I started wondering if I could give up on them and become a Cardinals fan. Obviously I did, starting in 2000. And it caused much 'discussion' (grief) among my friends and family who are Cubs fans. They always told me I'd be back following the Cubs when they did well. And 2003 taught me I was a true Cardinals fan, as I was – for a while – so terrified the Cubs really were going to make it to the World Series as things progressed in the playoffs."

As for the night of Game 162 in 2011, I asked Christine what she would tell her grandkids. "I'd tell them it was a night that reminded me why baseball is

the best sport and why I love it so much. It
exemplified the beauty of the game itself – anything
can happen on any given night, and an absolutely
amazing convergence of 'anythings' happened in four
incredible games."

•   •   •

Daniel Shoptaw, 36, is an influential presence in
Cardinalsville via podcasts (the weekly "Gateway to
Baseball Heaven" on Seamheads Podcasting Network
and as a regular contributor to the UCB Radio Hour
produced by Ivie League Productions), blogging and
Internet forums (CardsClubhouse, United Cardinal
Bloggers, Baseball Bloggers Alliance), and Tweeting
(@C70). He was born in Little Rock, Arkansas, and
now resides about an hour up the road in Russellville.
In what some of us call real life beyond the realms of
baseball, he serves as an accountant.

Shoptaw recalled, "The night of the 28th, I spent a
lot of time on the phone refreshing Twitter, talking
about the game and all that was going on in baseball.
Of course, the Cards game didn't provide much
drama, though I remember a lot of Twitter talk about
pulling Carpenter before his time at bat (since he
came up with a 5-0 lead) and saving him for the Wild
Card tiebreaker game, if there was going to be one."

Pessimistic Braves fans might be surprised at the expectations of a diehard Cardinals fan: "Once the Cards had won their game, I tried to keep up via various means on the Braves game as well as what was going on in the American League. There was less tension, though. I knew the Cardinals were playing the next day, at worst. All through this run, I had been enjoying the ride but not necessarily fully investing in believing they could come back. I was pretty sure that they were going to have to play another game, because Atlanta was going to win."

And yet, as with the baseball world at large, Shoptaw marveled at the long and winding road his Redbirds had traveled (or "flown above," if we are worried about appropriate metaphors). "It was almost incomprehensible. It didn't seem possible that these Cardinals, left for dead at the end of August, were going to the playoffs. The American League was an afterthought, though I do remember checking the phone before going to bed and seeing the Rays had snuck into the playoffs as well."

The marketing folks at Wiffle Ball (invented and made in the U.S.A., still!) would be pleased, albeit not surprised, at the ubiquitous appearance of their product in baseball folklore. "I started following baseball late, around seventh grade, and so I didn't play any organized baseball. I'd often go out in the backyard with a Wiffle Ball bat and Wiffle balls or a wooden bat and tennis balls and play my own imaginary game. I'd play occasionally with my father and my little brother, but not all that often.

"I saw some Cardinal games when I was just beginning my teenage years. I remember going on photo night, where the players came around and you got to take pictures of them. Which is how I got my picture taken with my favorite Cardinal player, Ozzie Smith. Two years ago, we actually ran into Ozzie at his St. Louis restaurant and my son got a picture with him, which was even greater!"

How does one explain the trajectory and timing of baseball events on September 28, 2011? "I don't know if you could explain that night to someone that didn't understand baseball. You had to know what was going on, what was at stake, what the odds were that one of these major comebacks could work, much less two. It's a night I'm not sure baseball fans even have completely wrapped their head around!"

•   •   •

As an eyewitness in Houston, Tony Bender confirms some of the hunches Dathan Brooks had about the number and volume of Cardinals citizens at Minute Maid Park on September 28, 2011. Bender, who moved to Houston in 1997, was born into a family of Cardinals fans in deep Southern Illinois, lived in Springfield, Illinois while the Class A Midwest League team was there, and went to St. Louis a couple times a year to watch games.

Despite being a Texas resident, Bender frequents the virtual hallways and lounges of the popular Viva El Birdos, or VEB, blog, at vivaelbirdos.com, as TBender, and he scouts out Cardinalate activity on Twitter, Facebook, and STLToday, the *St. Louis Post-Dispatch* website. I asked him if he is related to Charles Albert "Chief" Bender, the National Baseball Hall of Fame Native American pitcher credited by some as the inventor of the slider. Evidently, he is not related to our Hall of Fame Mr. Bender.

Bender chronicled the scene he witnessed in Houston, noting, "Local Cardinals fans are always excited to see the team play. We were confident that at the very worst there would be another game in St. Louis on Thursday (Game 163). 'We take of business today and worry about tomorrow tomorrow,' one guy wearing a Bob Gibson jersey said as we all milled about before the game. And the group of us standing there all agreed with him.

"After that first inning, I knew the game was over," Bender continued. "From the moment Chris

Carpenter stepped out of the dugout he seemed
focused, determined, unhittable. He's an intense
player normally, but that night his mannerisms were
more intense, of someone with more controlled anger
and competitiveness. He was on a mission. It was the
kind of night where you felt you were going to see a
no-hitter."

Growing up, Bender played some manner of baseball
from T-Ball through his junior year in high school.
His father had played ball at a small college in
Tennessee and was offered a contract, but didn't sign.
He has been told that his first game was at Busch
Stadium, in 1977, at less than a year old, but his first
game memory goes back to 1983, in Kansas City. "I
saw Boston play the Royals. That was Yaz's last year
and he DH'd. George Brett played third base for the
Royals. John Tudor, later of the '85 Cardinals, started
that day for Boston, but KC won. I have a picture in
my mind of the fans cheering Yaz, the fountains in
the outfield, KC winning, and the nice ladies sitting
next to us who gave me cookies."

Bender offered a you-are-there perspective on the fine
art of pennant-fever scoreboard watching while a
game is in progress: "From my perch in the upper
deck behind home plate, I saw lots of folks doing as I
did – checking the scoreboard constantly and
commenting on the Philly-Atlanta game. Cardinals

fans cheered every Philly run. We noted every Atlanta zero. Carpenter's early dominance calmed me down so much that during most of the actual St. Louis-Houston game I was watching him pitch in between scoreboard checks and following the Philly-Atlanta game on my phone. Fortunately, the St. Louis offense and Carpenter's pitching took care of most of our immediate worries so we could watch to see if Philly could come back from the 3-1 deficit they had early in their game."

The excitement for Bender began after the Cardinals' 8-0 victory. "I saw few non-Cardinals shirts as I moved downstairs after the game. I had hoped the Houston folks would put the Philly-Atlanta game on the big screen since it was still going on, despite starting an hour earlier. They didn't, which wasn't unexpected. But a hundred or so fans crowded around the Cardinals dugout to cheer the team and hope they would get to celebrate with us. The team didn't, but Carpenter did come out to do a TV interview and he seemed pleased with the night's performance. After he finished the interview, he waved to us and ran back to the clubhouse to watch the other game. Meanwhile, Astros personnel began herding us out of the stadium. So we all had to leave, but no one wanted to go home."

Bender said, "We did what any reasonable person would do in that situation: we went across the street and took over the bar. There are a couple of bars across the street from Minute Maid Park, and they became home to a large contingent of Cardinals fans who had been at the game. I went into the Home Plate Bar & Grill and squeezed my way into a space so I could watch the other game on the big screen. They had the three other games on various TVs around the place. So many of us packed into the place they had to open the upstairs bar."

Our Cardinal fan in Houston recalled hearing raucous chants of "Let's go, Cardinals!" or "Let's go, Phillies!" at the bar, with the crowd growing, supplemented by some watching from the outside through the windows – all in Cardinals gear.

"And then Philly loads the bases in the ninth. They tie the game. We cheer! Atlanta walks the bases loaded. We anticipate. Next guy retired. We sigh, but we still feel good because Game 163 is in St. Louis, and there is a report on Twitter that the Cardinals are already heading back home, which turns out to be false. I'm now hoping for a 16-inning game that burns Atlanta's bullpen. Most of us are only half watching the American League Wild Card games, but every once in a while a table next to where I was standing points out that the Yankees and Rays are still playing and that Boston can't put away Baltimore. So some of us started peeking at those games, just in case. A cheer did go out when Dan Johnson's improbable home run tied the Yankees-Rays game and that game then went into extra innings."

Bender continued, "As the extra innings went on, we were concerned about every Atlanta at-bat. We cheered every Atlanta out. We worried about every Atlanta base runner. You could hear folks saying, 'C'mon (insert Philly player's name here)' or 'Bear down, Philly!' as if the Phillies were their favorite team. The bottom of the twelfth inning was excruciating, as Atlanta's potential winning run in Jason Heyward was wild-pitched to third base. A huge sigh of relief swept over the bar when the third out of that half-inning was recorded. 'Let's go, Phillies!' started up again, as it seemed the momentum had just shifted in their favor. Somewhere in the extra innings, the Twitter feeds told us that the Cardinals were still in the visitors' clubhouse across the street, lockers covered in plastic and eyes glued to the TV. I said to a guy wearing a throwback powder blue Jack Clark jersey, 'Man, I wish we could be over there watching this.' He agreed and bought me a beer – my first drink of the night, as I don't drink at the games since it is so expensive."

Bender described the frenzied finale in the thirteenth inning and its celebratory aftermath. "Philly gets a baserunner! 'Let's go, Phillies!' Then two outs. Single

to right. 'Let's go, Phillies!' And here comes Hunter
Pence, former Houston Astro and man with the
goofiest looking swing since Willie McGee. He hits a
dying quail…that falls for a hit and Philly leads! Our
chants seamlessly switched from 'Let's go, Phillies!' to
'Let's go, Cardinals!' Jumping, hugs, high fives,
rounds attempting to be bought — that poor
overwhelmed waitstaff. And then Atlanta gets their
chance. The nervous calm returned because Atlanta
was sending up the heart of the order against
somebody named David Herndon. Jones strikes out.
Uggla walks, and we get more nervous. Then,
groundball to Howard, who throws to Rollins — out!
— and then the relay back to first — out! I shouted
out the play like I was scoring it: THREE! SIX!
THREE!"

Although Bender's team had won its way into the
postseason, capping a historic comeback September,
his night as a fan contained a few bonus surprises yet
to come. "We were too pumped to call it a night. So
we stayed, and watched the insanity unfold on the AL
side. And as it did, we all cheered — except for the
lone Red Sox fan. Everyone knew we had just seen
the greatest night in baseball ever. The 45-minute
drive home did nothing to slow me down, so I turned
on the TV, fired up the laptop, and flipped back and
forth between ESPN and the MLB Network. I

collapsed at about 2 a.m. and I went into work late on Thursday."

· · ·

We close our Redbird Recollections with another eyewitness rendering, a celebratory missive from Chris Mallonee, of North Austin, Texas. He was eager "to get all of this down again so I don't forget the best night in baseball history!"

Mallonee, 29, is a fourth-generation Cardinals fan who grew up in Southwest Missouri and moved to Austin after college in 2005. He works at a software-as-a-service company managing the production and accounting departments. "I married a beautiful East Texas girl named Laura. She's a die-hard Astros fan, but my love for the Cards and her love for Berkman have her coming around to the good side." During the 2011 season. Mallonee started the birdsonthebat82.com blog. The "82" represents the year he was born, which just happened to be a year the Cards won a World Series. Shortly after starting his blog, he became a part of the United Cardinal Bloggers and began hosting the UCB Radio Hour once a month with Dathan Brooks.

"The radio gig started when Laura and I were driving back from visiting my parents in Missouri the night after the 2011 All Star game. I was extremely bored because there was no baseball on. I found the UCB podcast, listened to it, and loved it. I found the UCB guys on Twitter and asked if I could be a guest on the show. Dathan said I might as well co-host one episode with him. Have been doing it ever since. I never would have dreamed that in a few months from co-hosting that first episode, I would have been on shows interviewing Matthew Leach and Jenifer Langosch (Cards beat writers), Jim Hayes from Fox Sports Midwest, Cardinals prospects Trevor Rosenthal and Garret Wittels, among others. The 'new media' have opened up possibilities for fans that never existed before, and it is absolutely tremendous."

Mallonee also writes a weekly column on the Cardinals for i70baseball.com and a Playing Time Today column and a minor-league column for baseballhq.com.

"Close to 11 p.m. the night of the 27th I decided I would take half a day off of work and travel to Minute Maid Park to watch the season finale knowing that the Cardinals could force at least a playoff game with the Braves. My wife, Laura, brother Nathan, and high school buddy Ryan, from Dallas, decided we were all going to the game. We agreed to be at the ballpark when the gates opened at 5 to watch batting practice and get good seats. I have never seen a sporting event have more or cheaper tickets than that game at MMP. I was a little surprised that more people wouldn't come out for the last game of the Drayton McLane ownership era, as well as a game that had playoff implications. I bought four outfield tickets for two bucks apiece and we ended up sitting 20 rows behind the Cardinals third-base dugout."

Mallonee recalled, "I had caught word through the cybersphere that Cards fans would be out in force for the game, but I had no idea the extent to which that would be true. We stopped for a quick bite in LaGrange, Texas, and saw two other families in Cardinals jerseys headed to Houston for the game. We were two hours from the stadium."

When the Mallonee contingent arrived around 4 p.m., they went for a pregame snack and brew across the stadium and found it packed with Cardinals fans, "outnumbering 'Stros fans at least 5 to 1. Then there was the one poor guy in the bar wearing a Cubs hat. He took it from both groups of fans there."

The group entered Minute Maid Park when the gates opened and walked down to the Cards dugout to watch batting practice. "I was surprised at how loose the team was before such a big game. Octavio Dotel came over to the stands and chatted with what I presume to be people he knew from his time playing in Houston. The guys were focused but loose during BP.

"Watching that game was a surreal experience. Loud cheers would erupt for the Cardinals and hardly anyone would cheer for Astros (not that the Astros gave them much to cheer about that night). It seemed to me at least a 6:1 or 7:1 ratio of Cards-to-Astros fans in the building that night. The few Astros fans sitting in our section were getting annoyed by the constant conversations going back and forth about the scores of the Phillies-Braves, Yanks-Rays, and Red Sox-Orioles games, but we didn't care.

"I bought a battery pack for my iPhone before the game realizing I would have my MLB At-Bat app running the whole time, and didn't want to run out of juice at a critical moment. I became the guy in the section keeping everyone updated on all the happenings in the Braves game. It was a blast."

Mallonee says three moments from the game are etched in his memory: the number of fans taking pictures for every Albert Pujols at bat, Lucas Harrell pitching in the seventh inning for the Astros, and the bottom of the seventh when the scoreboard posted the Braves-Phillies score. Mallonee explained that Harrell's father, Brad, was his American Legion coach in high school. Lucas Harrell, who is three years younger than Mallonee, played high school baseball against Mallonee's brother. "Last I remember him was as a young boy throwing baseballs against a fence on a field adjacent to cow pastures in Rogersville, Missouri. Now I was watching him pitch in a major league game against Lance Berkman. My worlds had officially collided."

When the stadium scoreboard operator changed the Phillies score from a 1 to a 3, to show they had tied the Braves, Mallonee reported, "A huge cheer erupted in the stands. Carp paused before his next delivery and turned and looked at the scoreboard. From where I was sitting, I could see David Freese and Nick Punto, and I will never forget the smile that crossed their faces."

Mallonee felt his team was on the brink of the playoffs. "Watching Carpenter's face coming off the field in the seventh and eighth innings, I would have predicted snow that night a more likely occurrence than Carp giving up a seven-run lead."

When the game ended, Mallonee was within feet of the Chris Carpenter ("Carp") interview with Jim Hayes of Fox Sports Midwest. "I was right there when he was walking back into the dugout and tipped his cap to the crowd. If you would have asked me who

I would take in a Game 5 of the NLDS between Carp and Halladay, I would have taken Carp 10 times out of 10 just based on his death stare I witnessed that night."

Mallonee remembered Cardinals fans taking up the chant "Happy Flight" and yelling for the stadium to put the Phillies-Braves game on the video board. The group reluctantly left the stadium and headed across the street to Home Plate Bar and Grill, which was so packed with Cards fans that "our group of four could barely get in the front door to see a TV screen. We made it through the bottom of the twelfth before we had to head back to Austin. As I was driving and listening to the game, my phone was blowing up with texts and Tweets. I had to make a quick pit stop to pick up soda and snacks when I heard that the Phillies had beaten the Braves in the thirteenth. I walked back to the car, looked at my brother, and we both just sat there. After a couple of moments, he said, 'Chris, do you realize we were a part of the greatest night in baseball history?'"

Chapter 7
Tomahawked

"Every wave, regardless of how high and forceful it
crests, must eventually collapse within itself."

Stefan Zweig

Only in retrospect did this night of baseball take on
the "where were you?" communal quality of landmark
events. Only after the full weight of collapse and
miracle was felt did people start to ask each other,
"Where were you when that happened?" As for the
Atlanta Braves and their fans, during much of
September and during their Game 162 against the
Philadelphia Phillies, they might well have sung a
refrain from a 1966 song by the Grass Roots: "Where
were you when I needed you? Where were you when
I wanted you?" Those wants and needs applied to two
things: clutch hitting and clutch pitching.

Pregame post by Ben Duronio, at the Capitol Avenue
Club, a Braves blog:

> So while today is the end of this season, it will
> also serve as the beginning of another season.
> Whether it be the post-season or the off-
> season, this is both an end and a beginning.
> The Braves get a fresh slate after today — or
> tomorrow if a playoff is forced — and while
> we will never forget how awful and
> tormenting this September was, we may wind
> up remembering 2011 for a different reason
> once October concludes. Thanks for the great
> season, Braves, fellow bloggers, and fans. Talk
> to you on the other side.

Before the game, the Braves exuded a quiet tenseness.
Thirty-nine-year-old Chipper Jones, the lone active
Brave from the 1995 World Series championship
team, delivered a pep talk in the dugout before they
took the field. His charges listened attentively and
clapped when he was done. Meanwhile, as events
cheerfully unfolded for the St. Louis Cardinals in
Houston, the Braves had enough to keep them
anxious in Atlanta. (Meanwhile? "Meanwhile" can be
the Personal Identification Nomenclature, the PIN,
the too-obvious password, for a ticket to the drama of
September 28.)

william holt @william_hotunc
Cmon braves. All I ask is one win. #praying

At 7:19 p.m. EDT a Ryan Howard double in the first
scored the speedster Hunter Pence, who had walked,
putting the Phillies up by a run. Keep in mind that
Phillies' skipper Charlie Manuel played his first string,
not scrubs, except for Shane Victorino, in a game that
was meaningless to him and his team's fortunes. Since
the Phillies had so handily won the National League
East, Manuel had rested his regulars. One could
reasonably argue that his use of the regular starting
lineup for Game 162 was a tune-up for the
postseason. To his credit – and perhaps to his dismay
once the playoffs began – Charlie Manuel employed a
starting lineup that consisted of Jimmy Rollins SS,
Chase Utley 2B, Hunter Pence RF, John Mayberry Jr.
CF, Raul Ibanez LF, Placido Polanco 3B, Carlos
Ruiz C, Joe Blanton P. The Braves, up against the
wall after losing 12 of their previous 17 games,
countered with Michael Bourn CF, Martin Prado LF,
Chipper Jones 3B, Dan Uggla 2B, Freddie Freeman
1B, Brian McCann C, Matt Diaz RF, Jack Wilson
SS, and Tim Hudson on the mound. Atlanta tied the
score in their half of the first on a single by Bourn
followed by a stolen base, an advance to third on a
fielder's choice, and a sacrifice fly by Chipper Jones at

7:27 p.m. Things remained quiet until the home half of the third inning. The Braves' Michael Bourn singled and stole second. Martin Prado followed with another single. Atlanta tried a double steal with Chipper Jones at the plate. Bourn was called out in a close play at third (it would have been his third swiped bag in the game), and when Jones struck out, it looked as if the Braves' threat had fizzled. Bourn was irate. He tore off his helmet and argued the call with umpire Dan Iassogna, joined by his skipper Fredi Gonzalez. The Braves claimed Bourn's left foot reached the bag before Polanco's tag. Replays seemed to support their contention. But the Braves were not to be denied. Dan Uggla followed with a two-run homer off lefty Cole Hamels, who had come in to relieve Blanton in the first relief appearance of his Major League career. The 413-foot-long blast to left field was Uggla's 36th of the year. The crowd, announced as 45,350, had something to cheer about. Maybe a month-long, season-ending collapse, after all, could be avoided. It was 8:03. The Cardinals' game at Houston was just about to get under way. Keep in mind that Atlanta and St. Louis began the night with equal records. If Atlanta won, they would end the 162-game schedule tied with the Cardinals, at 91-71. In that event, the Braves would have to travel to St. Louis for a one-game tiebreaker. But if the Cards won and the Braves lost, the season would end for Atlanta.

well good for the Braves... so far. I'm one Phillies fan
who has always liked the Braves from way back to
Aaron and Matthews.
Laurence via MarkBowman.MLBBlogs.com.

The Braves' 3-1 edge held until the top of the seventh.
All the while, any Braves scoreboard watcher could
see that the Cardinals' out-the-gate 5-0 lead against
the Astros had held up. In the top of the seventh,
Raul Ibanez hit a one-out double to deep right center
off Tim Hudson, followed by a Placido Polanco
infield single, putting runners at first and third.
Carlos Ruiz reached on an error by shortstop Jack
Wilson, allowing Raul Ibanez to score at 9:07 p.m.,
trimming the lead to 3-2. Wilson's error was costly
and memorable. It likely replayed in the heads of
many Braves fans over a long winter. Hudson was
finished, leaving with a line of 6.1 IP, 6 H, 2 R, 2 ER,
1 BB, and 4 K. Eric O'Flaherty came in and got
Shane Victorino, batting for Vance Worley, to hit
into an inning-ending double play. Braves fans could
find reason to rustle a bit in their seats. It appeared as
if the Braves might escape, might cling to a 3-2
victory, buying time, buying another day. In a
foreshadowing of a mess that Craig Kimbrel would
get into in the ninth, Jonny Venters got into an
eighth-inning jam by means of a pair of walks

sandwiched around a hit batsman, Ryan Howard, to
fill the bases with two outs for Ibanez, but Venters
struck him out swinging on three pitches. End of
inning.

Rookie phenom Craig Kimbrel was called on to save
it for the Braves in the ninth. Kimbrel, who would go
on to be selected unanimously as the 2011 National
League Rookie of the Year, had a streak of 38
consecutive scoreless outings over 37 2/3 innings,
striking out 67, allowing 14 hits and 11 walks. That
run ended September 9. The Braves bullpen – and
especially Jonny Venters and Craig Kimbrel — had
been sensational through August, but they had begun
to show human frailty. In a brutal loss to the New
York Mets, on Sunday, September 18, Venters had
walked in the tying run, followed by a go-ahead single,
and to rub salt in the wound Kimbrel gave up a rare
homer (only his second of the campaign) in the ninth.
With all the Braves' hopes on the line in this game,
Kimbrel gave up a single to right from Placido
Polanco. Pete Orr, whom I had seen play in Syracuse
in the minor leagues, came in as a pinch runner. The
Braves' closer then struck out Carlos Ruiz swinging.
One out, one on. Ben Francisco came up to bat for
pitcher Ryan Madson. He took a strike looking,
followed by three straight balls. Francisco swung to
make it a full count, and then Kimbrel lost him, a
walk. Runners on first and second, one out. Kimbrel

walked Jimmy Rollins on seven pitches to load the bases. Then Chase Utley lofted a fly ball to deep left, scoring Orr on a sacrifice fly. The game was tied at three. It was 9:56.

Hudson deserved better. He pitched great after the first inning.
JD via AJC.com.

Phillies fans John and Donna Winner had flown down from Philly for the game in Atlanta, as they do two or three times during the regular season. They have found they can take in an afternoon game and return to their New Jersey home by the next morning. In attendance for Game 162, the Winners, whose name cannot escape making an editorial comment to other fans on behalf of their beloved Phillies, sat about seven rows behind the Phils' dugout in Atlanta. "It seemed as if Kimbrel was in there one batter too long, at least," remarked John Winner to me in a mid-winter phone conversation. "You could sort of see his rookie-ness written all over his face." Winner related how nearby Braves fans in the stands were nervously scanning scoreboards, iPhones, Blackberrys, Androids, and other assorted drumbeats from the social media jungle. "When Kimbrel collapsed, you could just feel the floor drop out of the place," recalled John Winners. More curiously perhaps, our on-the-scene witness noted how despairing Braves fans in the ballpark began to root against the Boston Red Sox and for the Tampa Bay Rays. As they followed out-of-town events on the scoreboards or smartphones, they sought some sliver of salvation by rooting against the fortunes of the Red Sox. It was as if the collective Atlanta fan base was always murmuring, "We do not want to be known for the worst-ever collapse. And if we do, we don't want the spotlight of shame. May the Sox lose and the Rays win, so we can lick our wounds quietly, or at least share the pain." Or, who knows, maybe somewhere deep in the Hegelian collective Jungian unconscious, Braves fans remembered their own Boston connection and could not help but be united in apocalyptic gloom with their American League former counterparts?

Guys, we've got a lot of young talent. A lot of guys who need more time out there and will surely be great players for years to come. Even if we win this game and tomorrow we are probably relegated to looking towards the future.
not_the_old_nc via MarkBowman.MLBBlogs.com.

After Kimbrel walked Pence to load the bases again, manager Fredi Gonzalez had had enough. Of 29 pitches thrown, 16 were balls. Kimbrel, who would set a rookie record for saves, would not be able to manage one more. Gonzalez brought in right-handed reliever Kris Medlen, who had been out most of the year recovering from elbow surgery. Medlen got Michael Martinez to pop out in foul territory by third base. Further damage was averted. At 10:11, Jack Wilson, who had a chance to redeem himself from his error, struck out to send the game into extra innings. The Cardinals were almost finished with their victory, so any scoreboard watching took second fiddle to what was transpiring on the field at Turner Field. The Braves, who had held a lead through most of the game, were on the cliff. Medlen efficiently disposed of the Phils in the top of the tenth, getting a groundout, a flyout, a single, and a strikeout. Facing Michael Schwimer in the bottom of the tenth, the Braves went quietly, managing only a Michael Bourn single to left. At 10:33, Michael Martinez caught a Chipper Jones fly to deep center to send the increasingly tense contest to the eleventh. Atlanta brought in reliever Anthony Varvaro to face the Phils in the eleventh, and he allowed two walks (one intentional) and a Chase Utley stolen base, all harmless. In the bottom half of the eleventh inning, Schwimer handily dispatched the home team, striking out Uggla, getting Freeman to line out to short, and inducing a McCann groundout to second. As any veteran baseball fan knows, an extra-inning affair is fraught with extreme possibilities. It can settle in to a tense, almost prosaic interval that gets its own groove. Sometimes, with relievers depleted, position players take the mound. (Not likely in such an important game.) Managers get to show their game skills as illustrated by how they orchestrate their depleted resources. All the while, though, one error, one hit by a sneaky bench player, one costly mistake, can reverse all expectations. The top of the twelfth exhibited more of the lull, the coiled spring, with righty reliever Cristhian Martinez keeping the Phils at bay and maintaining the Braves' hopes. Mayberry Jr. singled, but Martinez got Ibanez to hit into a double play, with Wilson Valdez grounding out to shortstop to end the Phils' turn. But the Braves came tantalizingly close to snatching a win in the bottom of the twelfth. With Justin De Fratus (remember the name) relieving for Philadelphia, Jason Heyward singled to right and Jack Wilson bunted to the pitcher, sacrificing Heyward to second. Pinch hitter Brooks Conrad struck out for the second out. Michael Bourn was walked intentionally, putting Braves runners on first and second. When De Fratus uncorked a wild pitch, Heyward advanced to third. The winning run was 90 feet away. But Martin Prado grounded out to third and the threat ended. It was 11:13. Scott Linebrink came in for Atlanta to pitch the thirteenth. On the season, the veteran had recorded one save and seven holds, finishing the season with a 3.64 ERA, 42 strikeouts, and a WHIP of 1.45. Linebrink promptly struck out pinch hitter Domonic Brown and then walked Brian Schneider. He then got Jimmy Rollins to fly out to center. Two outs. Chase Utley singled to right, putting runners on first and third with two outs. Then Hunter Pence, "with the ugliest of swings producing the ugliest of hits," in the words of Sports Illustrated's Tom Verducci, followed with a broken-bat scorcher to the right of Freddie Freeman and just out of reach of second baseman Dan Uggla and too far in for rightfielder Jason Heyward. Pence's single scored Schneider and gave the Philadelphia Phillies a 4-3 lead. The scoreboard clock read 11:28, but none of the fans worried about the hour. It was the score that mattered. Utley advanced to third on the play, but he remained there as Linebrink got Michael Martinez to foul out. The damage was done. Technically the Braves still had a chance, but they looked defeated. Rookie David Herndon came in for the Phils in the bottom of the thirteenth, striking out Chipper Jones swinging, walking Dan Uggla, and getting Freddie Freeman of Atlanta to ground into a 3-6-3 double play, ending the game, eliminating the Braves, and enshrining a place for the Braves in the Hall of Memorable Collapses. (Numerologists might claim something inauspicious in 363, such as symbolizing how close the Braves came to completing their year, as in 365 days. I know, I know, I'm reaching here.) The Phils won 4-3 at 11:40.

Momentum, ours it was not.
So many opportunites wasted, can't win like that.
NCChopper via TalkingChop.com.

David Herndon earned his first career save, Justin De
Fratus won his first game, and Scott Linebrink fell to
4-4, and the Braves were in shock. As Linebrink, now
with the World Champion Cardinals, joked to St.
Louis Post-Dispatch reporter Derrick Goold in
spring training 2012, "I feel like I played a little bit of
a part in that just with the collapse we had over in
Atlanta." But more seriously, he reflected, "It was
crazy. It was like a three-week car wreck, watching it
in slow motion. ... We ran out of gas, and it was hard
to watch knowing how good we were for 5 ½ months."

I know you guys probably don't want sympathy from
a Phillies fan but, your team still played hard all
season. It was never a "breathe-easy" moment for the
Phillis [sic], until halfway through September. On the
bright side, your bullpen still kicks ass, despite the
Blown Save and what not, you still only gave up 3
runs in over 9 in nings, and one was because of an
error on your backup shortstop, another because of a
broken bat bloop hit barely out of the infield...

Philly Greg via TalkingChop.com.

Their tableau of defeat featured Dan Uggla on his knees like a penitent, Freddie Freeman with head in hands, and Brave after Brave and fan after fan staring vacantly in disbelief. For Atlanta, a long, hard winter had begun a lot sooner than any calendar had ordained.

MLB @mlb
Did that really just happen? Best night of baseball ever? RT this if you are fired up for the #postseason

Justin Shaddock @jshaddo
"oh no, I don't want anymore Braves or Red Sox gear." –kid in Africa

Miran Maric @miranmaric
Come on, Atlanta... We started out so strong this year, only to collapse at the end of the season... We'll get 'em next year... #Braves

---

Chapter 8

Winter Comes Too Early

"People ask me what I do in winter when there's no
baseball. I'll tell you what I do.
I stare out the window and wait for spring."

Rogers Hornsby, quoted in *Baseball and the Meaning
of Life*

Did all of America feel the pain of "America's
Team"? Owing to their cable television ubiquity, Ted
Turner and WTBS marketed the Atlanta Braves as
"America's Team" in the late 1970s and early 1980s.
It is debatable whether the proposition that the
Braves are America's team caught on, either as a
signature name or as a national team to root for.
Nevertheless, the Braves can make a singular
geographical American claim: they are the only
franchise in Major League baseball to win a World
Series as a home team in three different cities: Boston
(1914), Milwaukee (1957), and Atlanta (1995).

If a team is not demonstrably representative of one nation across time zones and regions, is it possible that its fans share a "personality"? Does cumulative collective experience show itself in similar attitudes and gestures? If you accept either of those premises, then Braves fans, wherever they are, might be seen as a blend of loyal, genteel, resigned, and rebellious – with perhaps a dash of sweet tea or barbecue sauce. But I am neither a sociologist nor a Southerner, so any conclusions about the fan base run the risk of portraying a stereotype.

Let's hear from an anecdotal sampling of Braves fans to help you form your own conclusions. Our cadre of ardent Atlanta followers includes several who attended a whole bunch of games at Turner Field, including That Game on September 28, 2011.

Katie (@Katiebravesfan) is a nanny, 33, originally from New Jersey, who moved to Atlanta in 2007. She lives in Sandy Springs, Georgia. She attends 60 or more Braves home games at Turner Field and watches maybe 90% of the road games on TV. Annually she likes to make one trip to spring training, a road trip, and some trips to minor league AAA venues. She chats up the Braves with friends in "real life," on Facebook, and on Twitter but does not have a blog and tends to avoid reading others' blogs. During the season, she spends a fair amount of her

time on weekends hanging out with other fans
outside of Turner Field trying to get players to sign
autographs.

"I had been feeling disappointed and nervous for the
team for over a week. The night of Derek Lowe's loss
I burned a Derek Lowe card in the parking lot with
some fellow fans. We were pissed at him for his shitty
season. He could have had one more win. If he had,
we might not be in such a tight race.

"The night we were eliminated? I remember thinking
I was going to be sad either way because I hate the
end of the season and not seeing my 'baseball family'
for a few months. I just had a sneaking suspicion that
we were going to lose."

Katie typically sits on the 300 (club) level. On
September 28 against the Phillies, "I just couldn't
watch the game. I went to get in line for a snack,
and there was a TV where I could watch the game. I
was talking to the woman in line in front of me about
how the season was just done for, and the man
behind us joined in the conversation. It was Otis
Nixon [switch-hitting speedy center fielder, 1983-99;
two stints with the Braves; famous for a remarkable
1992 catch] and he had hope that they would pull out
a win."

"I eventually walked down to the field level and found a friend of mine to sit with. She was in the same mood as me. We had given up hope and knew a loss was coming. When we did lose, she and I kind of stared at the field for a while. We watched the dugout clear out except for pitcher Brandon Beachy. He stood there leaning against the rail for a good 10 minutes. He looked how I felt — shocked."

Katie resented the Phillies' decision to play their starters despite already having the comfort of a playoff spot. "Was it to make us look like fools? I remember thinking that they put their starters in to make us lose, which would backfire cause the Cardinals had the only winning record against them and they would send the Phillies home. I was right!

"After the game, my friend and I did our usual thing. We went to the street next to the players' parking lot to watch them leave. Players came out and left, some quickly, some slowly, some in cars, some in cabs. We were glad to see they looked as disappointed as we felt. It was after 2 a.m. when the last player left."

She retraced her first visit to Turner Field, in 1997. "I remember everything about that day. What I wore, who pitched, who they played, who won, what I ate.

Even though the Braves lost, it was a great day and a great memory!"

And months later she still smarted over the loss that sealed the Braves' 2011 collapse. "I don't think I'll ever really talk about that night again. Part of my heart died that night. No matter how great or how bad the Braves seasons are in the future, I will never forgive that team for the pain they put me through."

•   •   •

Martin Gandy runs the Talking Chop blog about the Atlanta Braves and has more than 4,000 followers of his @gondeee Twitter account. Talking Chop logs upwards of 10,000 or more regular visitors a day, from throughout the continental U.S., Hawaii, Alaska, Canada, Japan, China, and Australia. Gandy is a computer systems engineer in his mid-30s, living in downtown Atlanta, within sight of Turner Field. AtIanta-born and -raised, he went to college at the University of Georgia in Athens (UGA).

"My first MLB memory is going to a card signing at a baseball card shop in Marietta, Georgia, called Baseball Buddies. If I recall, I got Jerry Royster's autograph. I go to my fair share of games, both Major League and minor league. I actually prefer attending minor league games during the bulk of the season —

they are more personal and feel more like real baseball than the corporate entertainment of most Major League games," Gandy related in an email.

On the night of September 28, Gandy was at home, pacing around in front of the TV, yelling a lot, exasperated a lot. "But over the past week I had seen it coming, like the Nothing, consuming everything in its path; inevitable and unstoppable. The most frustrating part was the Braves' inability to hit, to string together hits, and to get key hits in critical situations. At the end there was no Atreyu to save the Braves."

Gandy said the fact that the Red Sox one-upped the Braves' collapse just a few minutes later numbed the pain a bit, but he was by no means rooting for the Red Sox' collapse.

"I couldn't watch much baseball after that. And this was kind of the story of the Braves run of 14 straight division titles with only one World Series. In so many of those series they played the team on the hot streak, and the Braves were the team struggling to hold it together."

Talking Chop consumes a large portion of Gandy's day, usually in little chunks. A dedicated core of bloggers helps out on the site, handling day-to-day matters such as game recaps and series previews during the season; this leaves him free to highlight important or interesting stories. Gandy says he modeled Talking Chop after the blogging style of Andrew Sullivan, using quotations to evoke responses, and responding to news at it happens, while trying to involve readers.

When asked how he would tell future generations or someone who did not follow baseball about the collapse, he replied, "I would use this collapse to tell people that saying something will never happen, doesn't mean it won't happen. At the beginning of September I was more than certain the Braves would make the playoffs. I was using phrases like 'sure thing,' and 'in the bag.' My optimism, and the optimism of all Atlanta fans, took a solid punch in the gut on the 28th of September."

• • •

Lauren Turbyfield provides a female fan perspective via @BravesLove, with its more than 1,000 Twitter followers and at her blog at Lovemybravos.com. She has run the blog since September 2007, garnering visitors from all states (the most visits from Georgia, Alabama, and Tennessee), and 145 countries. Outside the U.S., the greatest number of visitors come from

Canada, Australia, and the U.K. She attended 50 games in 2011 and blogged about them all.

"I grew up here in Atlanta and have been a Braves fan forever. When I was 3, I had a Dale Murphy number 3 jersey! Murph was my first favorite player. He was a great role model and, by all accounts, a great teammate.

"As a superficial and quick conclusion, I've detected Braves fans as being more resigned and less bitter than Boston fans regarding their respective collapses. That's not to say Atlanta's accustomed to losing. Sometimes I think the South cares more about college football than they do about their own children. Generally speaking, professional sports are not as important to the fans. 'Ho hum, the Braves are in the playoffs again. Want to go to a game?' 'No, I have a project at work I really need to finish up. Besides, the game's at the same time as the Georgia-Florida game. Do you think I'd miss that?' Once college football starts in the South, the Braves are sort of forgotten, especially if they're not in first place.

"There is definitely a core group of fans who want to be there for EVERYTHING. Every big game, every Friday Night Fireworks, every autograph signing. Their desks at work are covered in bobbleheads and their bulletin boards covered in ticket stubs. They wear their Braves shirts as regular clothing, not just game day wear. The team — as much as it changes on an annual basis — becomes more than a hobby. It's like family. I'm pretty sure I saw my favorite parking lot guy, ticket taker, security guard, and usher more than I saw my parents last summer.

"But when the last game was played I didn't have overwhelming feelings of heartbreak, sorrow, or anger. I'm a spectator. I can't change the situation, and I don't feel like the Braves 'owe' me as a fan."

Lauren grew up just west of Atlanta and lives in Atlanta. Her father remembers watching the Atlanta Crackers (before the Braves came to Atlanta in 1966). Her parents met when her dad and uncle were playing on an adult traveling softball team. The boys became best friends, her father thought her mom was pretty cute, and they have been married more than 40 years.

Baseball permeated Lauren's family life. A different uncle was scouted as a pitcher. All the cousins in her age group were male, and they all played baseball. Family get-togethers always included getting the ball and gloves out, seeing who could get the most "pop" from the leather. Her brother was a state all-star pitcher/centerfielder in Little League and played a couple of years on the same team as Matt Capps, the

Twins' closer. Everyone either played baseball or softball, and if they weren't playing, they were watching the Braves.

"My first MLB memory would be sitting in the super-nosebleed right-center seats in Atlanta Fulton-County Stadium. Those were the only tickets my dad could afford, but the place was so empty we were often able to sneak down behind home plate. When I took a pretty bad spill on my bike when I was 7 or 8, my dad told me if I'd stop crying (read: hyperventilating) he'd take me to see Tommy Glavine pitch. I dried up immediately! Glavine was always my favorite of the big 3."

As for September 28, 2011, Lauren was at Turner Field. "I try to be a confident fan — was telling all my stadium friends to stop saying goodbye, that I'd see them on Tuesday! — but I didn't lose my confidence until Scott Linebrink came in. He was sort of Fredi's white flag all season. Kimbrel and Venters were so tired. It was easy to see from the fan perspective, although they both denied it.

"We kind of knew it was coming. The Braves were running on fumes in September -- just look at our record. Our offense was dead, our pitchers were tired, key members of our bullpen were overused, and it was catching up. I remember Jonny Venters insisting in interviews that he wasn't tired, that he just wasn't making the pitches he wanted. But to watch him...he was taking deep breaths before every pitch. His face looked tired. It was like it was taking all his energy to throw one more pitch... then one more... then one more.

"I don't think Kimbrel was as tired, even though he made almost as many appearances. I do think he got a little caught up in his records and all the talk over his eventual Rookie of the Year award. He's a young guy; I didn't expect him to be level-headed. Actually, you don't want a closer who's level-headed. You want a beast out there in the ninth.

"I had trouble sleeping after the game not because the game was lost, but because I just wanted to hug all my Braves and tell them it's okay, everyone's tired, it's not entirely your fault, the season wasn't lost on the final day, and because I always have a crash of depression when the season ends. I love my team — what am I going to do for the next five months?"

•   •   •

Josh Gralton (@gralton) is a 24-year-old college student and soccer coach/aspiring teacher from Dahlonega, Georgia. He's been hooked on the Braves since he was 10 years old, taking in spring training

and attending as many as 50 games a year. He says
the team consumes his daily life, whether they are
doing well or poorly. His follows the Braves by
keeping up on team news and chatter equally during
the season and the offseason. He considers himself a
Braves source, one who has scooped more staid and
traditional national sources of Atlanta Braves gossip
or information. Gralton's Atlantainsight.com blog
covers the entire local sports scene and boasts a loyal
following.

Josh describes himself as an autograph hound. He was
featured in an *Atlanta Journal-Constitution* article on
"how to get an autograph from a Brave"
(http://jgwb.us/bravesauto). Gralton also calls himself
a "huge pessimist" with respect to the Braves, citing
the team's record of one World Series championship
during a string of 11 straight Eastern Division titles
from 1995 through 2005.

"As the season got closer to the end, I would analyze
the schedule and try to figure out what exactly we
needed to do to get in the playoffs. You could feel the
team wearing down. You could see they were in one
of the typical season valleys, and it wasn't looking
good. Nothing was clicking on offense, and the
pitching was starting to struggle. I remember
thinking on September 8, when the Braves had a
series against the Cardinals in St. Louis, 'All right, we

have a 7.5 game lead with 18 to play. If we go 7-11 (91-71) and St. Louis goes 14-5 (90-72) we win. There's no way we don't win 7-8 more games with 12 more against the Marlins, the Mets, and the Nationals. The team is in a funk but not bad enough to have the train fall off the tracks, so to speak.' Then we go and lose 7 out of our next 9 ballgames, so I start to look at everything again. We have 14 to play with a 4.5 game lead. We have this."

Gralton remembers his dad taking him to his first ballgame at Atlanta-Fulton County Stadium when he was about 8 years old. "He told me we were going out to eat and surprised me. I fell in love that day with the game — the sounds, the players, the stadium, the food, the total atmosphere. One day when my dad was taking me to school, he didn't go the right way. He handed me a newspaper that had the spring training schedule on it (I was about 11). He said, 'We are going to Florida. Pick the games you want to go to, it's up to you.' I have been a huge baseball fan ever since. I used to lie and say I was going to the movies, and actually head to the ballpark when I first got my license, sometimes by myself."

Asked to describe his take on The Night of the Collapse, Gralton said in an email, "I had tickets to the game. I chose not to go. I didn't want to be there, in all that emotion.

"Then the unthinkable happens. It's over. Atlanta is owned by Philly. And it's not one of those situations where you start to hate them because of a rivalry — because it wasn't. They just beat us. They aren't obnoxious, they don't talk a lot of trash, they just play hard-nosed, good baseball. You could feel we weren't going to win the game. You could see it on their faces."

He continued, "The wheels fell off. I really felt numb, a strange feeling, not really rage. We were just feeling, 'We don't deserve this. It's not meant to be, it's just not meant to happen.' I did root for Boston to lose. I didn't want the media to rock the Braves alone."

As for any enduring legacy from this game and this night, Gralton offers a sunny optimism that bravely tries to hide a wound. "I wouldn't bring it up again. The past is past. Focus on the good times. Even that day wasn't really so bad in the big picture. Chances are we were probably only going to play three or four more games anyway."

• • •

A third-generation Atlantan, Craig Patterson, 42, lives 1.5 miles from Turner Field. Although born and raised in Atlanta, he has lived in a few other places — Park City, Utah, and Louisiana—but he keeps

coming back. He works as the communications
person at a renewable energy company whose focus is
commercial growing of an energy grass.

Patterson recalled a step-grandfather who faithfully
watched the Braves on TBS and took him to his first
Braves games, which at the time was "way downtown,"
about 45 minutes away. "I was at the game when Pete
Rose had his [44-game] hitting streak broken by the
Braves. We rooted for Bob Horner and Dale Murphy
amid all the buzz about 'Charlie Hustle.' I was also at
game 12, when the Braves tied the opening winning
streak record (to be broken and set at 13 wins). I still
have the cardboard handout they gave to all the
attendees."

Patterson has us fast-forward 25 years, and we find
him with a son of his own. "Baseball is a shared
experience for my son and me. I don't have much to
go on with how to have a shared experience between a
father and son, but baseball is fitting the bill nicely as
we've both found a natural rhythm between us with it."

The Braves and baseball have become an instrument
of bonding for Patterson and his young son. "I live
close to the Braves' Turner Field. My son Sam has
become a fan. He loves the experience, even if his
desire to watch each and every nuance of play is still
developing. Where once he would want to spend the

entire game in the Cartoon Network Braves Playhouse (Tooner Field) and shopping for sugar and ballpark souvenirs, he now can sometimes sit for a whole game — or almost a whole game. During a mundane sixth inning, I'll sometimes look over at him and appreciate this fact as he chants 'Let's-Go-Heyward clap-clap-clapclapclap.'

As for September 28, 2011, "Sam and I went to each of the closing series games against the Phillies, though each was a school night. Sam had become quite a fan of our incredible bullpen, especially Craig Kimbrel. We had, in fact, found a favorite spot in 2011 next to the bullpen in the outfield where, just before each game, the relievers would chat with and sign for kids at the wall. Sam was a proud supporter of Kimbrel, Jonny Venters, Eric O'Flaherty, Kris Medlen, Julio Teheran, and had signed balls as tokens of that.

"We watched the last game of the season and marveled at how the Ted was really rocking. Red foam tomahawks rippled all over the stands. To me, having been there for the Braves' attendance highs in the Nineties, it brought back memories of when Atlanta sold out every game."

Patterson sent me this piercing bit of dialogue, preserving for us the precious perspective of a 10-year-old:

Me: "Sam, do you remember the Braves' last game?"

Sam: "Of course."

Me: "What do you remember?"

Sam: "I remember Uggla hitting that home run and the place going crazy. I remember being hoarse on the way home. I remember leaving because we had the lead and Kimbrel was coming in, and we were going to the playoffs."

Patterson continued, "Sam and I did, indeed, leave. Two straight days of staying up late for the games during school nights had my wife on edge about school performance and we had to get back to get Sam to bed. Kimbrel had a lead. He never gave up leads. The Yankees were killing the Rays in the seventh. The Orioles were down to the Bosox. All seemed set for a play-in game on 9/29 for the Braves. So we left. I had the game on the radio on our short drive home. Kimbrel lost the lead before we got home. Extra innings. Sam went to bed. I watched the rest unfold after that. Incredible night and all that..."

And then the hard part: "I had to tell Sam the Braves lost the next morning. His little hoarse voice said: 'Really? Really? It's over? What will I say to Joe? To Mark?' His face had fallen a few millimeters. Mark, the Phillies fan in his second-grade class, and Joe, the Yankees fan, were indeed going to be brutal. I felt for him. I couldn't change it for him. I felt helpless. But then I realized that this was a lesson in fandom. His life was going to be full of ups and downs as a supporter of a team. Dealing with crushing turns, piled on by jeering fans of other teams, was going to be a part of being a fan. He was about to get a real big dose of that, in a really severe way, having been a part of one of the most devastatingly brutal few weeks of baseball Atlanta has ever seen."

Sam survived, and is stronger for it. In the winter of discontent after the Braves' fall, Patterson watched his son. He gauged Sam's support for the Braves and wondered whether his baseball heartbreak would cool his passion for baseball. "I'm proud to see that it has not. He's as passionate as ever. He wants to go to spring training. He wore his Uggla and Chipper jerseys throughout the winter, just with long sleeves underneath. He's still a fan, I'm still a fan. We're both stronger fans. We're a bit closer. I can't help but think that 9/28 was an amazing night professionally and personally, as my son and I will remember it forever, with both spite and with fondness."

Chapter 9
Precursors of Fate

"Fate is never fair. You are caught in a current much
stronger than you are."

Cassandra Clare, *City of Ashes*

We can only consider the Red Sox at Orioles game in
the context of its twin, the Yankees at the Rays.

And the Yankees are starting the one, the only Dillen
Betances at pitcher tonight. In the words of Jack
Currey from YES, odd pressure situation. Game
means nothing to Yankees, a lot to the kid &
everything to Rays/Sox. Our chances are riding with
Betances!
Rick via JoyofSox.com.

For each of these games, think of the Scoreboard as a Tenth Man in the lineup of the Red Sox or the Rays. (Or is that the 11th man? As a National League fan who resists the Designated Hitter, I get confused.) The Red Sox lineup featured Jacoby Ellsbury CF, Dustin Pedroia 2B, David Ortiz DH, Adrian Gonzalez 1B, Ryan Lavarnway C, J.D. Drew RF, Marco Scutaro SS, Carl Crawford LF, Mike Aviles 3B, and lefty Jon Lester (15-9) as starting pitcher. The Orioles countered with Robert Andino 2B, J.J. Hardy SS, Nick Markakis RF, Vladimir Guerrero DH, Matt Wieters C, Adam Jones, CF, Mark Reynolds 1B , Chris Davis 3B, Nolan Reimold LF, and righty Alfredo Simon (4-9) pitching. The Red Sox entered the game at 90-71, while the Orioles stood at 68-93, almost mirror images of success and futility. But that only tells a statistical story and does not show the momentum of the previous month or the arc of this game on the night of September 28, 2011. At 7:10 p.m. Alfredo Simon threw his first pitch against the Red Sox in Baltimore. The game's first few innings were uneventful with no runner in scoring position except Baltimore's J.J. Hardy, who doubled in the first with one but was stranded after Lester got Markakis to fan, looking, and induced a Guerrero groundout to third. In the third, Alfredo Simon walked Boston's Mike Aviles and yielded a Jacoby Ellsbury single to left. At 7:49 the Red Sox took their first lead of the night on a Dustin Pedroia single to center, sending home Mike Aviles. A more substantial rally was thwarted when Simon got David Ortiz to ground into a double play and got Ryan Lavarnway on a swinging strikeout. Lavarnway was an interesting story in his own right. Not only was it rare to see a philosophy major from Yale in the big leagues, he was also one of baseball's few Jewish players. He tore up Ivy League pitchers, setting Yale and league records, including a 25-game hitting streak. He put up sensational offensive numbers throughout his minor league career, and was called up by the Red Sox on August 18, 2011, to fill a roster spot for the injured Kevin Youkilis (coincidentally also of Jewish background). Most notably, on September 27, the day before the season finale, Lavarnway made his debut as a starting catcher, replacing the injured Jason Varitek and Jarrod Saltalamacchia. He belted two home runs and drove in four runs in leading the Red Sox to a crucial 8-7 victory over the Baltimore Orioles. Lavarnway's performance enabled Manager Terry Francona to go with the hot hand and keep him as the starting catcher for Game 162, subject naturally to second-guessing after the fact.

Hercules (Larvarnway) come slay the bird again tonight!

fusionmouse via JoyofSox.com.

The Boston 1-0 lead did not last long. In the home half of the third, Lester walked Chris Davis on eight pitches, forced Davis on a Reimold fielder's choice groundout, with Reimold advancing to second on an Andino soft groundout to third. Then Lester tried to get a 91 mph fastball by J.J. Hardy, who smashed the ball to left for his thirtieth home run, scoring Reimold and giving Baltimore a 2-1 lead. It was 8:06. The Bosox promptly tied the score in their next at bat with the benefit of a Scutaro double, with Crawford moving him to third on a groundout to short. With Aviles batting, Simon balked home Scutaro to tie the game at 8:20, but Boston ran itself out of taking the lead when Aviles was gunned down by catcher Matt Wieters in an attempted two-out steal of second. The Red Sox, however, did regain the lead on Dustin Pedroia's twenty-first home run, about 390 feet to left center, in the fifth, giving Boston a 3-2 lead at 8:36. Ortiz singled off the rightfield wall, chasing starter Simon (4.1 IP, 6 H, 3 R, 3 ER, 3 BB, 2 SO), and Adrian Gonzalez managed a single against Simon's replacement, lefty Troy Patton, by safely getting to first on a ball deflected off Patton to second baseman Andino. The Red Sox had runners at first and second with one out. But Patton got Lavarnway to line out to left and J.D. Drew to fly out to Adam Jones in center.

Baltimore escaped with a one-run fifth inning. Once again, the Sox squandered an opportunity to extend their lead.

The tenacious Orioles would mount their own threats, more than once. In the bottom of the fifth, Mark Reynolds would make it to third on a leadoff double and infield groundout. Reynolds tried to score on a Nolan Reimold grounder to shortstop Scutaro, but he was tossed out at home on a rocket throw from Scutaro. Big out for the Red Sox.

Jim Rome @jimrome
Seriously, twitter is going to break tonight. And it's going to be MLB not the Shield that busts it.

And in the bottom of the sixth, the Orioles got to Lester for two walks to start the frame, only to have Vladimir Guerrero hit into a double play. Lester issued a third walk in the inning, to Matt Wieters, but averted damage by retiring Adam Jones on a strikeout (assisted by Lavarnway and Gonzalez).

Then the cosmos intervened. At 9:34 p.m., rain halted proceedings in Baltimore just so everyone in the Boston dugout and in New England and beyond could get fidgety and so that matters could ethereally

synchronize with events in Florida. The rain delay
was nature's way of casting more fear and doubt into
the hearts of Red Sox Nation as Tampa clawed back.
The rain delay entered the archives of baseball lore for
another reason. During the hiatus, *Boston Globe*
sportswriter Dan Shaughnessy made comments later
construed by some as a jinx. On NESN with Heidi
Watney, he said, "The Red Sox season is not going to
end. They live to play another day. The Rays aren't
going to come back from 7-0." The video clip of his
prediction on YouTube concludes with Watney
warning, "You never never say 'never.'"

Play resumed in Baltimore at 10:58. By then, in the
top of the seventh, manager Terry Francona replaced
lefty starter Jon Lester with righty Alfredo Aceves.
Lester, starting on three days' rest for the second time
in his career, had performed not superbly but
creditably, giving up four hits, walking four, striking
out five, and allowing two runs over six innings. He
had thrown 93 pitches.

But if you listened carefully you could hear the
spiritual galactic pulleys tightening and squawking
already with a few flinty sparks flying into the night.
All of this was written. Amid the rain delay in
Baltimore of 1 hour 26 minutes, Tampa tied its game
with the Yankees and the metaphysical and physical
weather in Baltimore had metamorphosed. To

paraphrase the poet William Butler Yeats, the center
of the Red Sox universe would not hold. The Red
Sox were slouching toward Armageddon. The death
march began in the top of the seventh. Pedroia
worked a one-out walk and Ortiz smacked a single,
advancing Pedroia to third. But Ortiz got nailed as he
tried to advance to second. Two outs. The Orioles'
Patton intentionally walked Adrian Gonzalez,
runners at first and third. New O's reliever Willie
Eyre forced out Ryan Lavarnway. And the Red Sox'
half of the inning was over. Two runners were left on
base. In the bottom of the seventh, Aceves hit two of
the first three batters he faced. Ouch. He escaped
further calamity, though, by whiffing Andino and
getting Hardy to ground out. Aceves had logged 7.1
innings in the last four days and performed valuable
duty. At least no loss was pegged on him. That would
not have fulfilled the appointed script of fate. In the
top of the eighth, O's reliever Pedro Strop teased the
Red Sox into thinking they could add to their lead,
but any clairvoyant could see that the baseball gods
and goddesses were merely toying with the
Bostonians. Marco Scutaro hit a one-out single
succeeded by a Carl Crawford double in the left-
centerfield gap that eluded the O's defenders.
Leftfielder Nolan Reimold's diving effort proved
futile, with centerfielder Adam Jones retrieving the
ball that had rolled past Reimold. All the while,
Scutaro was motoring, trying to score on Crawford's

hit. But a bullet from Jones to shortstop J.J. Hardy, who relayed a strike to catcher Matt Wieters, who applied a tag to the sliding Scutaro at the plate, ended the play. Out. It was 11:18 p.m. EDT. As if to shine a light again on Wieters, or to add some wattage to his name on the scoreboard, Mike Aviles popped out to the catcher Wieters to end the inning and erase another critical scoring chance for Boston. Fate, anyone? Boston did, however, still lead, 3-2, but it didn't feel like a lead. And what the heck was going on down there in Tampa? If Boston could manage a win, Boston was alive for a one-game tiebreaker, no matter what happened in Tampa. And vice versa. No matter what happened in Baltimore, if Tampa stayed alive and won their game, they were alive, period.

The bottom of the eighth was pedestrian, routine, and relatively easy, with Red Sox reliever Daniel Bard retiring Baltimore in order. The only scare was a Matt Wieters fly ball to deep right that J.D. Drew snagged in the corner for the final out.

The ninth was a different story. Oh, it was a different universe. Baltimore manager Buck Showalter brought in Jim Johnson to face Boston in the ninth, with Boston leading 3-2 but with a lead that was already smelling funny with the multitude of missed scoring opportunities. Showalter also shuffled his defensive alignment, taking out Nick Markakis and putting in

Matt Angle in left and moving Nolan Reimold from
left field to right field. The Red Sox were not about
to meekly surrender. Ellsbury reached on an error
from first baseman Reynolds and then promptly
swiped his thirty-ninth base of the year in Game 162.
A single to right by Pedroia put runners at first and
third with no outs. Red Sox fans had to be thinking,
okay, first and third, no out, we add a few insurance
runs, bring in our man Papelbon and the very worst
that can happen is we play one more game against the
Rays. Next, DH David Ortiz forced out Pedroia at
second. Joey Gathright came in to run for Ortiz. OK.
Runners still at first and third but one out now.
Johnson then intentionally walked Adrian Gonzalez
to load the bases, setting up a force play at every base.
Showalter was playing it by the book. And then, at a
time when Red Sox Nation felt confident of getting
at least one insurance run, Ryan Lavarnway hit into a
killer 6-4-3 double play, Hardy to Andino to
Reynolds, erasing Gonzalez at second and
annihilating a last chance to build their lead.

Naturally, Boston skipper Terry Francona brought in
his closer Jonathan Papelbon (I wonder if his name
anciently translates to "good-Pope-leaning-ish") to
shut down the O's and keep the season going for the
Sox. History was on the side of hope for the Red Sox.
After all, Boston had enjoyed an 89-0 record in
games they were leading in the ninth inning or later

up to this point in the 2011 season. Moreover, Boston's closer had blown only one save since May 9. It was 11:48 p.m. Papelbon struck out Adam Jones on five pitches. He then faced strikeout-prone Mark Reynolds. Strikeout-prone? More like strikeout-record-setting. Reynolds set a Major League mark for whiffs with 223 in 2009 while with the Arizona Diamondbacks. He led the National League in strikeouts in his first three seasons, and led the American League in his fourth full year. Papelbon served Reynolds four four-seam fastballs, the last three reaching 96 mph: called strike, ball, swing and a miss, swing and a miss. Strikeout. Two outs. All Papelbon had to do was get out one more Oriole as the bottom of the order came to bat. Boston had maintained its 3-2 advantage since the fifth inning. One more out to go, one more out to be guaranteed of playing a tiebreaker with Tampa as the worst possible scenario. Up stepped Baltimore's Chris Davis. Papelbon threw him one pitch, clocked at 98 mph, and Davis lashed it to right for a double, his twelfth of the season. Two outs, man on second. Bottom of the ninth. Showalter brought in Kyle Hudson to run for Davis. Then Nolan Reimold, who had gone 0 for 3 with a hit by pitch, faced Papelbon. Nolan Reimold, whose name summons thoughts of a pitcher, Nolan Ryan, not a hitter, took two balls from Papelbon and then swung and missed at two fastballs. Papelbon's face tempted Boston fans to summon memories of

collapses in 1978, 1986, and 2003 – at least for this
viewer. Down again to the last strike, the O's
Reimold unloaded on a 97 mph (some say 98 mph,
but what difference does it make?) Papelbon four-
seamer that was nearly a homer in hitter-friendly
Orioles Park. Reimold's ground-rule double to right
center knocked in Hudson to tie the game at 3. It was
11:59 p.m., a minute to midnight, and the game was
tied. For somebody it was Cinderella's witching hour
and for somebody else it was smashing pumpkins
time. Which would it be?

Jonathan Papelbon had thrown 16 pitches. Was he
tired? His pitches had shown good velocity, but did
they have movement? The reliever faced Robert
Andino, batting under the notorious Mendoza Line
(the eponymous epitome of weak hitting, after
shortstop Mario Mendoza, whose career batting
average is enshrined at .215, though the term gets
applied loosely and unfairly to this decent defender)
at .170, and a .196 average with two outs and runners
in scoring position. Andino had gone 0 for 4 with two
strikeouts in the contest but had scorched the Red
Sox for six RBIs in the last week. Papelbon started
with a rare offspeed pitch, a slider, to Andino, for a
ball. He came back with his trusted four-seam fastball,
for a called strike. On what appeared to be a split-
fingered fastball, Andino hit a flare to Carl Crawford
in left. How do we freeze-frame this and give it the

agonizing (or triumphant, depending on your loyalties) justice? Crawford got a glove on it, trapped it and dropped it, he just missed it, he could not handle the sinking liner cleanly, it was just out of his range. Take your pick. His throw home was meaningless. Reimold raced home from second for the winning run at 12:02 a.m. September 29 on the East Coast. Barely known Robert Andino's single had won the game for Baltimore, 4-3. The Orioles rejoiced as if they had won the World Series. They celebrated their sixty-ninth win as if it were their ninety-sixth. Technically, the Red Sox were not dead, but you could not tell that from the look on their faces. They knew they had collapsed. They knew they had not done their part to prevent their own collapse. Looking at it now, we know they had three minutes of breathing room left, but deep down they knew they were out of air. And there were no oxygen tanks within reach.

Andy Levy @andylevy
MLB should just cancel the postseason. Not gonna top tonight.

ESPN @espn
"We could be here for 100 years and NEVER see what we just saw." -@notthefakeSVP on @SportsCenter #MLB

CelticsLife.com @celticslife
If MLB teams were given an amnesty clause who
would Theo let go of? Crawford? Lackey? Personally
I won't be upset if Theo leaves.

After Boston's historic collapse, some pointed a finger
at Manager Terry Francona, saying he had lost
control of the clubhouse or that personal problems
interfered with his performance. Francona, whose
contract was not renewed in the wake off the debacle,
strongly disagreed with such characterizations. "You
never heard any of these complaints when we were
going 80-41 [from April 15 to Aug. 27] because there
was nothing there," Francona told Bob Hohler of the
Boston Globe. "But we absolutely stunk in the last
month, so now we have to deal with a lot of this stuff
because expectations were so high."

In a January 2012 postscript by ESPNBoston.com's
Joe McDonald, third baseman Kevin Youkilis said,
"We're a team and we lose as a team and we all failed.
There wasn't one player that didn't fail, because we
lost. We all failed."

Or as "Red" of the SurvivingGrady.com blog put it in
a day-after postmortem:

Think this one's gonna break me? You're
wrong.

I've lived through Bill Buckner. And Dave
Stewart shutting us down. And Roger
Clemens threatening Terry Cooney. And
1992's last place finish. And "Leading off for
the Sox in the 1995 ALDS, Dwayne Hosey!"
And Jaret Wright. And Kent Mercer. And
David Wells in a Yankees uniform. And
Aaron Boone. And David Wells in a Red Sox
uniform. And the Chicago beatdown of 2005.
And being a few plays away from making
back-to-back World Series in 2008.

So this latest breakdown? This collapse of
Jerry Bruckheimer proportions? This mind-
boggling implosion of one of the best team
ever assembled on paper?

Yeah, it hurts. It always hurts. But it's like
making out with a chick with German measles.
I've had my shots, baby. And I'm immune to
it all.

Chapter 10
Apocalypse Then

"Accept the things to which fate binds you, and love
the people with whom fate
brings you together, but do so with all your heart."

Marcus Aurelius, *Meditations*

The term "Red Sox Nation" describing the team's fan base reportedly goes back more than 25 years, to 1986, when *Boston Globe* writer Nathan Cobb reportedly coined it. Since then nearly every team and its fan base has employed "Nation" to affirm bonds of loyalty and wide appeal. But give Red Sox Nation its due: its citizens are fiercely loyal and united – sometimes bitterly — no matter where the baseball diaspora scatters them.

When the Boston Red Sox won their first World Series in 86 years, their fans celebrated the end of the alleged Curse of the Bambino. This was the name given to the superstitious belief that Boston owner Harry Frazee's sale of Babe Ruth to the Yankees doomed the Bosox all those years. The last great example of the so-called curse was Boston's loss in Game 7 of the 2003 ALCS to the hated Yankees, when Grady Little was their skipper. Little chose to stay with his ace Pedro Martinez after the tiring pitcher yielded three successive hits and a run in the eighth inning. A 5-2 lead was squandered and New York won in eleven innings. It was a crushing defeat after being five outs from a win that would have propelled them to the World Series.

SurvivingGrady.com is a popular, award-winning blog whose name underscores the keen sense of history that Red Sox fans exhibit, as well as their tongue-in-cheek dark humor. The blog gets about 50,000 unique visitors monthly during the season, less in the off-season. Loyal followers comment daily from Okinawa, England, and from across the U.S. The 2005 blog compilation, Surviving Grady, by Tom Deady and Tim McCarney celebrates the 2004 championship season. (To the blog community, Tom is known as Denton, Tim as Red.)

SurvivingGrady co-founder Tom Deady, 48, lives in Holliston, Massachusetts, a picture-postcard New England town that exercises traditional open-meeting government and serves as a charming residential community for many who work for the technology firms dotting Routes 128 and 495. A self-described computer geek, Deady is an IT manager who has worked with startups and other companies. He is a desktop manager overseeing a staff of 40 techies. As for Game 162, he followed the Red Sox and Tampa Bay games as a subscriber of the MLB cable TV package, switching virtually batter-to-batter between the two games. He didn't pay attention to the games in the National League. In a spirited and amiable phone conversation, he told me, "Going into that night, I had more or less written the team off five days earlier. You could see it coming. What really didn't shock me was Carl Crawford not playing in the right spot, not catching that ball for the final out." This sentiment echoes Bill Lee's take noted earlier, though with fewer mystical overtones. "I watched the replay of that probably a hundred times, and 99 of 100 times someone should catch that."

Let us pause here to note that on September 28, 2011, Mr. Deady was days away from his October 1 marriage to his longtime fiancée, Sheila Gray, now Deady. Preparations for that event are not known to have interrupted baseball-spectator activities of the evening in question.

When I noted how crushed the Red Sox looked after their loss to the Orioles, even though they were technically still alive for a Wild Card slot, Deady continued, "The Red Sox were defeated, even though an incredible five minutes remained before it was officially so. Their season was over the whole week leading up to that night. Francona was making the moves of a desperate man."

During the season, baseball is always on for Deady, if only in the background. He watches a lot of games, even watching the Yankees to root against them. Being a fan of the wider sport, he also likes to catch matchups of heralded pitchers, two Cy Young winners, for example, via the MLB package. Of course, he devotes significant time and energy to SurvivingGrady and spends a lot of time online. He attends an occasional game in person with Red, who runs SurvivingGrady with him. The SurvivingGrady gang typically meets at a bar once a year, such as McGreavey's in Boston. They also do an annual charity for the Jimmy Fund.

I like to ask people for memories of their first Major League game. For Deady, "It's a vague memory, except I remember how empty Fenway was, maybe in the Sixties. A clearer memory is the first time I brought my daughters, when they were around 7 or 8 years old. Just to see their faces when you come up the ramp. Everything is green, the field so green, just in awe. I hope I was like that." Deady's picturesque

description calls to mind Doris Kearns Goodwin's
Fenway Park portrait in *Wait Till Next Year* as she
returned to baseball after a long, sad absence owing to
her Dodgers' leaving Brooklyn: "There it was again:
the entrance up the darkened ramp disclosing an
expanse of amazing green, the fervent crowd
contained in a stadium scaled to human dimensions,
the players so close it almost seemed that you could
touch them."

In describing the 2011 season, Deady looks back to
the 1986 World Series, when the Red Sox famously
were within certain reach of victory over the New
York Mets. "I had a glass of champagne that had
been handed out. This seemed like those games. We
thought we were done with that kind of season. This
felt like any other season before 2004."

So, with resignation and stoic reserve, Deady
witnessed the final punctuation of a night and a
season.

"After Longoria's homer I flipped off the TV and
went to bed."

•   •   •

Baseball excites extreme passions. Neither rain nor
snow nor geography nor checkbook status holds fans

back when the moment of destiny arrives. That was true for me in 2010 when I hopped on a plane from Rochester, New York, to San Francisco just so I could breathe the same World Series air as my black-and-orange-wearing compatriots. Meet Tim Tribou, a 23-year-old Red Sox fan from Albuquerque, New Mexico, who flew to Baltimore for the season-ending series between the Red Sox and Orioles for his "first real self-funded vacation." At the time, Tim was the assistant guest services manager at a hotel in Albuquerque but would find himself unemployed by the time I was writing this. His parents' New England roots (dad, Maine; mom, Massachusetts) provided all the thread he needed to connect to the Boston Red Sox. Despite growing up and living in New Mexico, Tribou has proudly sported his Sox cap, wearing it to school, work, or even church.

"I had the idea to fly out to Baltimore when the Sox were still tearing through just about everyone they played. So I bought the tickets in August, booked my flights, and was pumped. About the same time my trip became official, the Sox began their epic slide into oblivion. I've been a true Sox fan since 2003 (yes, that 2003), and I was confident they could pull out of the nosedive they were in, catch fire like they had in May, and tear through the playoffs."

Tim Tribou's first MLB memory involves traveling
with his father and brother to Denver to see the Sox
play the Rockies in the middle of summer — in
freezing cold and rain, and maybe a touch of snow.
His earliest MLB memory altogether? "Mike Piazza
was a member of the Albuquerque Dukes, and we
were able to bring our own food into ballparks. He
saw us with our pizza and asked if he could snag a
slice. So we obliged." His work in the hospitality
industry enabled him to meet Jarrod Saltalamacchia
while he was with the Texas AAA club. And Tribou
recalls a "full-on conversation with George Kottaras
when he was with the Brewers AAA club. We had
the Red Sox game on in the lobby while he (and the
rest of the team) was waiting for their shuttles to the
ballpark. Wakefield was pitching for the Sox, and so
I said to him: 'You used to catch Wakefield, right?'
and he was like, 'Yeah.' And I was like, 'I bet that was
fun,' and he said, 'It was easy,' and I was like,
"Really?!' and he was like, 'Hell no, it was crazy!'"

Tribou recalled how the Red Sox had lost the first
game of the series on a ball hit by Robert Andino,
whom he had seen play in Albuquerque when Andino
was a Marlins AAA farmhand. Tim attended that
first game with his sister, who lives in Germantown,
Maryland, and attended the rest of the series by
myself.

"It all came down to the 28th. I had spent most of the day in DC and wound up being a little late. Prior to the rain delay I was far up on the left field side. Still excited beyond recognition. I talked to some lovely folks on the train in who had come from Virginia to see the Sox. And I got more and more pumped. I don't remember too much before the rain delay. I know that we were up and I began to believe. We were up on the O's and the Rays seemed hopelessly behind on the Yanks. All was well. It had rained two of the three nights I went to games in Baltimore, and as it began to pick up, we were ushered out of our seats to the concourse. I couldn't decide if I wanted to take a rain-shortened win, or see the whole thing play out. In my head I decided I wanted to see it play out. I didn't want to hear people moaning that we won a cheap one."

Tribou said during the rain delay initially none of the televisions were showing the Tampa-New York game. They were showing the Phils at Atlanta. During the seventh-inning hiatus of nearly an hour and a half, "I was eating ice cream and telling people I was taking their seats as they left the park, and I overheard some O's fans talking about the Yankees, how their lead was slipping. I felt the pinch there. I said, 'No way New York blows a seven-run lead to the Rays in the last game of the season. NO WAY.' The delay ended and I moved down to the third- base side, much closer to the field. By the time we were moving back into our seats, the Rays were moving closer to crushing my spirit. As we were settling into our seats, Dan Johnson was stabbing a knife into our collective chests. All we needed to do was win, and if nothing else it gave us one more game of baseball."

Young Tribou confessed what many of his fellow fans intuitively feared: "Every single Red Sox fan in attendance had a sinking feeling that something was going to happen. We were still up when we came back from the rain delay, but it was a small lead. We all know how it ended for the Sox: Andino sends one past a sliding Crawford, and the O's score and celebrate like they just won the goddamn World Series."

Tribou continued: "The Red Sox fans did their best to escape the taunts, but it was to no avail. I was outside the park when another cry rose from the stands after Longoria hit the bomb that ended our season. O's fans gave us hell for it. I shouted at one of them, 'At least we still finished with a winning record,' which may have just come out, 'WINNING RECORD!'"

• • •

Joy of Sox. Great name for a blog on the Bosox, with its play on words with *The Joy of Sex*, the best-selling book of several years ago, which itself played off *The Joy of Cooking*. The Joy of Sox blog was founded by and continues to be nurtured by Allan Wood. "I was born in Burlington, Vermont in 1963, and discovered the Red Sox when I was 11. I moved to New York City – enemy territory – in 1987. Being there in 2004 made that October extra special! My wife and I moved to Ontario, Canada, in 2005."

As for September 28, 2011, he told me, "I watched at home, via the Extra Innings baseball package. For several years, I have had game threads on Joy of Sox, and there are a couple dozen people across North America (and sometimes the UK) that watch the game and post comments. It's a great group of people, ranging in age from 20-60. At the end of Game 162, there were about a dozen people in the thread. We had the NESN/Red Sox feed and I was scoring the game (as I always do). Many of us were also following the Rays-Yankees game and giving updates.

"The Red Sox led 3-2, but Ryan Lavarnway grounded into a bases-loaded double play to end the top of the ninth. Then Jonathan Papelbon struck out the first two Orioles before allowing doubles to Baltimore's 8th and 9th hitters, which tied the game. Then Robert Andino singled to left for the winning run.

We all flipped over to the Rays game – it was in the 12th inning – and then Longoria's home run ended our season. It happened so fast – the two games ended within four minutes of each other. I had been the voice of optimism throughout the entire month of September, arguing that there was no way the Red Sox would collapse. The odds were too great. It was tough. And then a day or two later, losing Terry Francona as manager, was another punch in the gut."

As a San Francisco Giants fan, I discovered that winning the World Series in 2010 exorcised a lot of old demons, a lot of terrible heartbreak from other years (e.g., 1962, 1993, 2002). And Wood echoed a similar sentiment: "Before 2004, I would have been furious, inconsolable, and unable to sleep for hours. But something unexpected happened after 2004. I am now able to watch the games and not obsess on losses, no matter how bad they are. Before 2004, I would get so worked up over each loss, because maybe that loss would end up being the one that kept Boston out of the playoffs. Each game was life or death. It was not healthy, and it got really bad in 2003 and 2004. But winning a World Series changed my brain. Beginning with the 2005 season, any annoyance at a loss I have is gone within a minute or two and then I'm ready for the next day's game. I could never have expected this to happen; but it's been a pleasant surprise."

During the season Allan invests significant time following the Sox: two or three blog posts a day, plus the game, and maybe half an hour after the game. Through his blog, he has met another Sox fan in the area, and they have gone to a few Blue Jays-Red Sox games and seen the AAA team in Buffalo. Other than that, Allan Wood's Red Sox fan involvement is typically all online, either through Joy of Sox or at Sons of Sam Horn, where he has been a member for 12 years.

Allan recalled his inaugural visit to Fenway. "When I was 12, my dad bought a bus-and-game-ticket package, and I saw Fenway for the first time in August 1976. A five-hour bus ride, an 11-inning loss, and a five-hour return trip! It was incredible. I absolutely love Fenway Park. I remember the contrast of the green field and the Wall with the red seats – and the sweet smell of cigar smoke."

As for any legacy or conclusion regarding Game 162 of 2011, he says, "Many people were knocked out by the crazy finishes that night, but I have a hard time seeing it as amazing, honestly. It was a crappy night that ended a very crappy month. But it was not worse than 1978, 1986, or 2003 – not even close. Winning championships in 2004 and 2007 softened the blow, for me. I cannot imagine someone who does not follow baseball understanding any of it. The personal involvement and emotional connection to a team day after day and game after game and season after season after season is hard to explain even to a casual baseball fan."

•   •   •

Ralph Quattrucci, 50, was at Camden Yards with his brother, John, 48. Ralph is a 30-year Maryland transplant from Massachusetts. He provided an eyewitness perspective of brotherly partisanship. "So there we were, first row, within eyeshot of Heidi Watney [then-NESN Red Sox reporter] and the Red Sox dugout. As is the case in Baltimore when the Red Sox come to town, the stadium was filled with many out-of-town fans, always an irritant to the Orioles crowds. John was nervously optimistic, chatting it up with all the Red Sox faithful all around us.

"While watching the game directly in front of us, we were also scoreboard watching the Yankees versus Rays game taking place at the same time. What was strange about that was hearing John reluctantly rooting for the Yankees.

"Here is where it got crazy," Ralph continued. "As soon as the game was over, the Jumbotron was playing the end of the Yankees-Rays game. Everyone in the stadium was focused on the video screen.

That's when John turned to me and said with his last ray of hope, "It's not over yet, because Tampa could still lose. Just as he finished that sentence, Evan Longoria hit a laser beam over the left field fence. The Red Sox season was over in a flash. Camden Yards erupted. I remember looking into the Red Sox dugout and seeing Terry Francona, and realizing that was probably his last game as the manager of the Red Sox."

Quattrucci returned to a theme that other Sox fans who were there have voiced: the salt-in-the-wound exuberance of the Baltimore faithful, "treating that victory as if they had just won the World Series. Even more painful when you consider they were in last place. But I understood them enjoying the misery that all the Red Sox fans were feeling at that moment. Then I looked at my brother John. I had seen the same look in 2003. We said nothing on the ride home."

• • •

Lori Ducharme was born in Worcester, Massachusetts, in 1967 — on the night of a Jim Lonborg victory. "Not that I have any memory of that. But I like to think that being born during the Impossible Dream season somehow linked me to the Red Sox for life. I left New England to go to college and haven't been back except for Christmases, weddings, funerals, and trips to Fenway (not in that order)." She lives just outside Washington, D.C., where she works for a federal agency. Her first-person reflection on Game 162 was one of the most vivid of those shared with me, and arrived courtesy of a shout-out by Tom Deady on the Surviving Grady blog.

"I was sitting in Section 338, first row of the top deck behind home plate. I thought it would be a beautiful view of an on-field post-game celebration.

"I attended the game alone — by design. Those last few weeks of the season had me in a perpetual bad mood, and I would have been very poor company during that series in Baltimore. I had been to the game on the 26th, and when Josh Beckett lost I was so mad that I opted not to go to the game on the 27th. I was in a bad mood all day on the 28th leading up to the game.

"I followed my usual routine — got there when the gates opened, and circled around to the outfield to photograph the players during batting practice. I hadn't looked at those photos until I started composing my responses to your questions — now five months gone by. They include several photos of the pitchers (Lackey, Beckett, Buchholz, Papelbon) laughing and joking around — which now just pisses me off."

Ducharme recalled not being confident about the game, not because of fatalism but because September had been a "total disaster that seemed to come out of nowhere. The pitching sucked beyond belief. I didn't trust anyone not named Pedroia, Ellsbury or Gonzalez."

Her personal history as a member of Red Sox Nation begins with the memory of arriving home from school on the afternoon of the Bucky Dent game in 1978, in time to see Yaz pop up for the final out. Two years later, her grandfather took her to Fenway for the first time on her thirteenth birthday. ("Bob Stanley pitched, Jim Rice hit a home run, Sox beat Cleveland 4-1.") "The '86 World Series crushed me. The 2004 postseason, no exaggeration, changed my life forever," she says.

She also recalls a game at Fenway seated next to four elderly people from Boston, England, who had never been to a baseball game. Trying to explain Tim Wakefield to them gave her a whole new perspective on just how foreign baseball can be to someone who has never seen it.

On September 28, Lori Ducharme observed the usual share of Sox fans throughout the park, but "more O's fans than usual for a team that was 29 games out on the last day of the season." She also registered her displeasure with the Camden Yards public address and video board personnel, frequently showing highlights or live look-ins of the Phillies-Braves game, but not airing any video of the Yankees' pounding the Rays in the early innings of their game.

"As for the Sox-O's game, it just never felt comfortable. Lester was on a three-game losing streak and had gotten shelled in his previous start, and it never felt like he was in control of this game. I vaguely remember there being some concern about whether he was even healthy enough to start the game. I had watched him pitch an extended bullpen session two days earlier, and he was working hard with the coaching staff to resolve something — it was unclear whether it was mechanical or physical. Anyway, that night he was up 3-2 after five innings, and the Sox fans in my section (including me) were unhappy that he came back out for the sixth. We were muttering about Tito [Francona] having too long a leash for him."

Baseball consumes some portion of every day for Ducharme. Her largely Internet-driven involvement includes chatting with friends about baseball, reading baseball blogs, participation in the Sons of Sam Horn online community, and watching at least 150 Sox games a year, live or on tape delay. "I take a vacation day every Opening Day. I schedule meetings around workday afternoon games so that I can listen at my desk. I spend a week at Red Sox spring training every year. And the moment the season ends, I start counting the days until the equipment truck leaves Fenway for Fort Myers."

"Lester survived the sixth, of course. But from the seventh inning on, it just felt like the wheels were slowly falling off. It just felt like there was some foreboding kind of Jaws-like soundtrack playing in the background. For starters, Alfredo Aceves comes on in the seventh and promptly hits the first batter he sees. Yikes. I sank a little lower in my seat. And then the skies opened up.

"During the rain delay I had to run for cover. The lightning was much too close for comfort, and there was metal everywhere I looked around me. I spent maybe the first half hour on the outer walkway of the upper deck, huddled under just-big-enough overhangs with a mix of Sox and O's fans.

"A little ways away from me was an enclosed lobby-like area, where elevators ran from the upper deck down to the main concourse. When the crowd thinned out, I made a run for the indoor space and found a seat on the dry floor. I was following the Rays-Yankees game on my phone. The rain delay coincided perfectly with their six-run eighth. When they scored the second run, I needed oxygen. What little hope I had started deflating. And naturally at this point the jerks in the Orioles booth decide to air the Rays-Yankees game on every TV in the stadium. Boom, 7-6 Yanks, with most of their starting lineup now sitting on the bench. Many not-nice things were said about Joe Girardi. The O's fans had their swagger back (irritating at that point because it was through nothing of their own team's doing)."

Ducharme's own history with rain delays in Baltimore was not a good omen. "The last rain delay I sat through at Camden Yards was the night in 2009 that the Sox staked John Smoltz to a 9-1 lead, and after the rain delay the bullpen blew it up in an epic display of fail. The O's came all the way back to win that one 11-10, and the Camden Yards crew still replays the video highlights of that game leading into the bottom of the ninth of every O's-Sox game. It's nauseating. So I'm a little scarred by the whole rain-delay-at-Camden thing, and that was definitely on my mind as I sat in the lobby, watching the Rays climb back and the rain pour down."

"When they restarted the game at Camden Yards, it was 7-6 Yankees. About the time Aceves hit his second batter of the inning, the Rays scored the tying run. You could just feel the air leave the stadium. Or maybe it just left the area immediately surrounding my seat."

She continued: "In the top of the eighth, we had a chance. Marco Scutaro singled, but then inexplicably (to my replay-unassisted mind) hesitated on Carl Crawford's double, and was tagged out at home. I just remember thinking, Carl Freaking Crawford finally delivers a meaningful hit on the last goddamn day of the year, and reliable-all-season Scutaro effs it up? Seriously? And although we left the inning with the lead, it just felt like it was gone at that point.

"I have no conscious memory of the top of the ninth. The box score tells me that we had the bases loaded against the last-place Orioles, and we couldn't score. If October hadn't gone the way it did on Yawkey Way, I might think that box score was a typo.

"So the bottom of the ninth didn't come as much of a surprise. That half-inning was like watching a movie. I don't remember it feeling real. I don't remember experiencing it, just sort of watching it play out on what might as well have been a giant screen in front of me.

"When Andino got the hit, I didn't say a word. I turned and headed for the exit. And the escalator hadn't reached the main concourse before the Rays scored their winning run (now displayed on the giant centerfield screen by our gracious hosts). I slunk off to my car, and drove home. No radio, no music, no sound."

•   •   •

The writer Stewart O'Nan is no stranger to Red Sox fans. *Faithful*, the best-selling chronicle of Boston's 2004 World Series year, shared with the world the online correspondence and real-life fan adventures of O'Nan and fellow fan and author Stephen King. Fans may have even spotted Stewart at Fenway, or for that matter at any number of Major League ballparks. O'Nan, 51, was born and raised in Pittsburgh, where he now lives. He grew up watching Roberto Clemente and Bill Mazeroski play in Forbes Field, remembering sitting in right field behind the wire fence and watching Clemente play the weird caroms. He went to the last games at Forbes with his brother ("a doubleheader against Ernie Banks and Billy Williams and the Cubs that we swept") and the first game at Three Rivers with his grandparents and parents. In subsequent years he would follow the likes of Willie Stargell, Dave Parker, Al Oliver, and

Rennie Stennett in Three Rivers Stadium, including World Series titles in 1971 and 1979.

O'Nan told me via a lively exchange of emails that he has always been a Pirates fan, and remains a loyal Red Sox fan. "I've got my NL and AL teams. Only once, in 1990, did it look like they might meet in the postseason, but alas, they both tanked. And last year's [2011] visit by the Sox was the high point of the year at PNC. The Bucs took two of three from the Sox, and I'll admit that I rooted for the Bucs in all three (my wife alternated, Sox-Bucs-Sox). If we were in Fenway, I'd have rooted for the Sox in all three. Of course, each of those two losses contributed to us (the Sox) not making the playoffs, but, as I've tried to impress on Terry Francona, they all count the same, so you've got to get them while you can."

O'Nan, whose award-winning fiction includes *Snow Angels, A Prayer for the Dying, Last Night at the Lobster,* and *Emily, Alone,* was named one of America's Best Young Novelists by Granta. He is also one of the most avid baseball fans featured in *Baseball's Starry Night.* "Of the Pirates' 162 games, I probably caught 120 between being there in person, watching on TV, and listening to the radio. And I would have caught more if I'd been in town in April, July, and half of August. On my website there's video of me catching a

Pujols home run." Enough said on O'Nan's baseball street cred.

Game 162 of 2011? "I didn't watch. Didn't really care that much. Once Clay Buchholz went down in June, the season was over. The Sox, like the Yanks and Steelers and Patriots, have put themselves in the ugly position of having to win it all or the season's a failure. With Dice-K [RHP Daisuke Matsuzaka] out, and John Lackey sucking all year, the Sox were already regularly starting Alfredo Aceves and Andrew Miller. Once Buchholz hurt his back, we added Tim Wakefield, so three of our five starters were officially well below Major League quality. We only stayed in the race till the last day because of gigantic years from Gonzo [1B Adrian Gonzalez], Ells [OF Jacoby Ellsbury], Josh 'The Chronicles of' Reddick [OF], and a monster second half by Dustin Pedroia. Really, we were eliminated in June but refused to quit. Realistically, the Rays had no chance of winning it all, having that anemic offense, so it's not like they deserved it either. No, the big prize was the Yanks' and Phils' to lose. And they did."

Although O'Nan no longer lives in New England, he maintains contact with several hardcore online friends who chew over Red Sox games. Besides attending Pirates' games in 2011, he managed to get to a Red Sox game and minor league contests of the Pawtucket

Red Sox, the Jamestown Jammers, and the Erie
Seawolves.

O'Nan takes the long view of the 2011 season,
putting it in historical context and lyrically reflecting
on baseball's place in a larger tableau. "By now
everyone's forgotten the 86 years without a
championship, just as everyone's forgotten the
Patriots' entire history through 2001. But what's
important, finally, to a true baseball fan, isn't the
ultimate outcome of the season — it's the season
itself, the day-in day-out emotions we experience as
the team goes through its ups and downs. The days in
the backyard or at the beach listening to the game on
the radio. The box scores and the standings, the buzz
around town. Did the team give us an interesting
summer? Were they fun to follow? Was it exciting?
That's more important, I think, than whether they
win it all. I mean, it's great when they win it all, but
when they don't, that doesn't mean it was a bad
season, or that someone needs to be fired. It's
baseball: you win some, you lose some. The beauty of
it is that tomorrow they'll play again."

• • •

We end the sagas from Red Sox Nation not from an
on-the-scene eyewitness but from the faithful in
Florida. Ken Preuss was not at either game, but

watched both the Sox and the Rays games on separate screens at the same time from his home in Oviedo, just outside Orlando. "Mark Bellhorn is from here, and is the first cousin of my sister-in-law," reported Preuss.

Preuss watched with his son Bennet. "We were watching the Sox game on NESN via the computer, and the Rays-Yankees game on the TV broadcast. It was devastating as a die-hard Sox fan, but what made it an extraordinary experience for me was that my 10-year old son decided to watch along with me - having never really paid attention to baseball before."

Preuss's email to me continued, "Seeing him experience the roller-coaster ride was amazing. Both games were one strike away from ending the opposite way, and watching him go from ecstasy to disbelief in the span of a single pitch brought back so many memories of my own childhood ('75, '78, '86).

"My son is now waiting for the season to begin in search of redemption. I believe the evening — while one of the most disappointing of my life — created a new lifelong baseball fan."

Chapter 11
The Stars Align

"I'm a poor underdog,
But tonight I will bark
With the great Overdog
That romps through the dark."

Robert Frost, *Canis Major*

Meanwhile.

Dirk Hayhurst @thegarfoose
You know, The #rays do a great job of nurturing a culture where any player believes he can be a hero. Who will it be tonight?

Meanwhile the Yankees scrubs were toying with Tampa while the flightless Orioles were winging it with the Red Sox. While National League subplots, or uber-superplots, were playing out, two other games, in the American League, were making their own marks, one steadily and one haltingly. At the Trop in St. Petersburg, Florida, in front of 29,518 paying fans, the Tampa Bay Rays and their $41,932,171 payroll (29 out of 30) were fighting for their life against the New York Yankees and their $196,854,630 (highest) payroll, as measured by ESPN. Lefty David Price (12-13) took the mound for Tampa Bay. Price had gone 0-5 in his last seven home starts. His counterpart was the Yankees' twenty-three-year-old Dellin Betances, a 6'8" 260-pound righty in his inaugural Major League start. Yankees manager Joe Girardi had not named Betances as his starter until the afternoon of the game. The Yankees starting lineup featured a few names as little known as Mr. Betances, since Girardi was resting several of his regulars for the postseason games they were already assured of. Most notably, he vowed to rest closer Mariano Rivera as well as relievers Rafael Soriano and David Robertson.

The starting lineup consisted of Derek Jeter SS, Curtis Granderson CF, Mark Teixeira 1B, Robinson Cano DH, Nick Swisher RF, Andruw Jones LF, Jesus Montero C, Eduardo Nunez 2B, and Brandon Laird 3B. The Rays started with Desmond Jennings LF, B.J. Upton CF, Evan Longoria 3B, Matt Joyce

RF, Johnny Damon DH, Ben Zobrist 2B, Casey Kotchman 1B, Kelly Shoppach C, and Reid Brignac SS.

Guided by their John Wooden-inspired manager Joe Maddon, the Rays were loose. Before the game, "The atmosphere inside those clubhouse doors was almost no different than it would be before some invisible game in the middle of June," according to Rays outfielder Sam Fuld, who gave an insider's view of the night for Grantland.com in February 2012.

Price's first pitch was at 7:11 p.m. In the top of the first, Price struck out Jeter looking, allowed a Granderson single, and got Teixeira on a fly to center. Then Granderson reached second on his twenty-fifth stolen base of the year. Granderson scored at 7:21 on an error by second baseman Ben Zobrist on a routine play that typically would have ended the inning. In the Rays' half of the first Betances got Desmond Jennings to pop out to Swisher in foul territory and then walked B.J. Upton and Evan Longoria. He crushed the Rays' scoring threat by striking out Matt Joyce and Johnny Damon, both looking. At 7:54, the Yankees' Mark Teixeira connected for a grand slam, giving New York a comfortable 5-0 lead in the top of the second inning.

Ken Rosenthal @ken_rosenthal
Not a good night for #Astros or @DAVIDprice14's
dog Astro. Both trailing, 5-0. #Rays #stlcards

It appeared the Yankees would coast to victory. At
this juncture in the proceedings no one really could
anticipate the charging drama poised to play out later
into the night. That is why a look back at Baseball's
Starry Night is deceptive. Only in retrospect would
we know the jolt of electricity that would rouse us
from curling into winter hibernation. At 8:35 in the
fourth inning a second home run from Teixeira, this
one to left off Tampa's ace and the game's starter
David Price, who despite getting pounded was still in
the game, upped the Yankees' lead to 6-0. When
Andruw Jones connected with a round-tripper to left
field off Rays reliever Juan Cruz in the fifth inning at
8:52 it seemed the Rays had hit bottom, now down 7-
0 to the visitors. At this point, let's be honest:
although they will now deny it, a healthy portion of
Rays, Yanks, and even Red Sox fans either went to
bed, changed channels, or left the Trop. A 7-0 lead is
a pretty safe bet. But they say you have to hit bottom
before you can change. If you consider the futility of
Tampa's offense for this evening thus far, you would
have to conclude that the boys from Florida were at
or near bottom. Desperately in need of some – any! –

offensive threat, the Rays batters proceeded to sleepwalk through their half of the fifth (one walk and no hits with Longoria ending the inning with a strikeout against Phil Hughes), managed a single and walk in the sixth, stranding Johnny Damon at second, and ended the seventh with runners at first and second with rookie Russ Canzler striking out as he pitch hit for Matt Joyce. Talk about frustration. The Rays were not even putting a hint of a dent into the Yankees' touchdown-and-extra point lead. Moreover, with the added pressure of the Rays facing elimination, all but their ardent supporters would've called it a night and a season, right? Not quite.

As the Red Sox and Orioles were in a rain delay that started at 9:34, the Rays came to realize "all the pressure was on them," meaning the Red Sox, as Tampa manager Joe Maddon revealed in a February 2012 "town meeting" with Ron (Diaz) and Ian (Beckles) of radio station 620 WDAE, the Sports Animal. Maddon recalled how emotions changed in nanoseconds, explaining that he thought the "rain delay would benefit us and it did." At 10:17, in the bottom of the eighth inning the Rays' offense registered a heartbeat, not a flat line, as they scored their first run. Johnny Damon had singled, followed by a Ben Zobrist double and Casey Kotchman being hit by a pitch by the Yankees' Boone Logan. The bases were loaded. Reliever Luis Ayala came in and

faced pinch hitter Sam Fuld. In "Game 162," Fuld's
first-person account for Grantland.com, he broke
down the at-bat. "Ayala threw me three straight balls
to start the at-bat. Then two I-can't-believe-I-just-
did-that-to-this-little-slap-hitter fastballs right down
the middle. I stepped out, figured more of the same
was coming, and envisioned hitting a line drive over
Nunez's head at short. Nope. Changeup. Seven times
out of 10 I would have swung and missed over the top
of it. But this time I saw it right out of his hand, and
knew it was a ball immediately. Wow. Never took the
bat off my shoulder and got one of the easiest RBIs of
all time." Fuld's walk scored Damon for the Rays' first
tally. The score was 7-1. Moments later Ayala hit
Sean Rodriquez, bringing home Zobrist, B.J. Upton
scored Kotchman on a sacrifice fly to Andruw Jones
in left, and now the score was Yankees 7, Rays 3.
Then at 10:23 Evan Longoria lofted his thirtieth
home run to left, scoring Fuld and Rodriquez. Out of
nowhere, out the depths, de profundis, as the
Psalmist says, the Rays were alive and kicking. It was
a ballgame. They had sent 10 men to the plate and
now trailed the Yankees by a run, 7-6. As Fuld noted,
the score had gone from 7-0 to 7-6 in 25 pitches.
Three minutes after Longoria's homer, at 10:26, the
Cardinals completed their 8-0 victory over Houston.
The Rays six-run rally fell just short of tying the game.
After Longoria's stunning blast, pinch hitter John
Jaso singled to right. Pinch runner Elliot Johnson

stole second, but Johnny Damon popped out to someone named Ramiro Pena playing second for the Yankees (not All-Star Robinson Cano) at 10:27. In the top of the ninth, the Rays brought in reliever Joel Peralta, who kept the momentum, or at least the possibility of momentum, going for Tampa Bay by shutting down the Yankees in order on a Brandon Laird pop out to short, a Ramiro Pena strikeout, and a Greg Golson fly out to left. (Stalwart Yankees fans may be hard-pressed to recall the names of these Bronx irregulars.)

While Boston and Baltimore were still in a rain delay, the Red Sox players could not have been cheered by what they were witnessing on clubhouse televisions. The Red Sox clung to a 3-2 lead while they were powerless concerning the Rays' rally. It almost certainly got into their heads, as Maddon conjectured it would.

In the bottom of the ninth, the Rays sent up pinch hitter Dan Johnson, batting .108, to bat for Sam Fuld, who had been productive in the eighth-inning resurrection. Johnson would face Cory Wade. In his WDAE 2012 spring training interview, Maddon explained that the choice of Johnson was not mere hunch or guesswork. The Rays knew Wade, having had him in spring training. They knew it was a tough matchup because of Wade's great changeup, which

fades away from batters. But as the score had
tightened, Maddon's strategy had shifted, going for
broke, as he put it. He turned to Danny (as Maddon
called him) Johnson specifically for his home run
threat, fully realizing that Fuld was more of a contact
hitter and in fact would've remained in the game if
runners were on second or third with less than two
outs. Johnson had never been a full-time regular with
any MLB team and had spent the 2009 season in
Japan with the Yokohama Bay Stars, hitting .215. For
the Rays in 2011, he had hit one homer, way back on
April 8, a dramatic shot that proved to be the game-
winner against the Chicago White Sox. Worse yet,
the Rays had designated Dan Johnson for assignment
on May 20, 2011, recalling him on September 14.
Maddon praised coach Davey Martinez for keeping
his bench players ready. Johnson took a curve for a
called strike, a changeup for a ball, and a fastball for
another called strike. The Rays were down to their
last strike. The left-handed-batting Johnson took a
Wade changeup for a ball and then fouled off a
fastball. The count was 2-2. Then he hit a line-drive,
343-foot home run to right field off the foul pole
(third-shortest of the season at the Trop, according to
ESPNStatsInfo) at 10:47, tying the game at 7,
continuing the improbable comeback in the night on
the last day of the regular season, as 962 miles away,
the Red Sox still led the Orioles 3-2. As Sam Fuld
remembered, "Now we were going to win. We knew

it." (Odd postpartum-from-the-bat painful fact: Indications are that the Johnson home run's final destination was the groin area of a right-field fan. Talk about taking one for the team! As of this writing, however, the baseball of the game-tying clout has yet to be located for purposes of enshrinement.)

ESPN @espn
Everyone just learned the name Dan Johnson. #Rays #TIEGAME

Ken Rosenthal @ken_rosenthal
Dan Johnson HR with #Rays down to last strike. 7-7 tie.

darren rovell @darrenrovell
Record amount of Tylenol PM to be used tonight? Think a lot of East Coasters are going to have a tough time going to sleep #MLB

In the top of the tenth Kyle Farnsworth came in and did what he was ordained to do: shut down the Yanks and keep the excitement going for the home half of the tenth. He struck out the side, getting Eric Chavez on a called third strike, striking out pinch hitter Jorge Posada, walking Chris Dickerson and Brett Gardner (intentionally) and striking out Austin Romine, looking. In the home half of the tenth, the Rays, facing reliever Scott Proctor, settled back to planet Earth, with B.J. Upton walking, Evan Longoria flying out to centerfielder Gardner, Jose Lobaton getting called out on strikes, and Johnny Damon striking out.

Fuld's account describes the Rays reserves watching in the food room with one large-screen television showing their own game and two smaller screens displaying the Red Sox game. "It felt like a sports bar, not a clubhouse. We were all just fans, powerless to control the outcomes of these two gripping games," he wrote.

JB Long @jb_long
Joe Maddon just clinched manager of the year. End of discussion. #Rays

---

Entering the eleventh inning, one sensed a loose Tampa Bay team exuding an air of "what do we have to lose?" This likely derived from the demeanor of manager Joe Maddon, who always had the deft touch, the right balance of severity and breeziness, sternness and levity. In the eleventh, Brandon Gomes made Maddon happy by dispatching of the Yankees on 16 pitches, inducing Eduardo Nunez to fly out to Upton

in center, Brandon Laird to left fielder Desmond
Jennings, and Ramiro Pena to whiff, on eight pitches.

In the eleventh, the Rays offered a ripple of hope for
sealing the deal by manufacturing a walk by Zobrist
[against Proctor] and a Brandon Guyer single after a
Kotchman flyout. But the incipient rally redux fizzled
when Sean Rodriquez forced out Zobrist at third on a
groundout to Eric Chavez and then Jennings popped
out to second baseman Pena.

In the twelfth inning, the Yankees added some
wattage to the electricity crackling in the Florida
night. Gomes gave up a single to Golson, which
prompted Maddon to replace him with Jake McGee.
The lefty had made his Major League debut against
the Yankees, in September 2010, walking three in 0.1
inning. In 2011, he had given up 5 homers in only 28
innings. Eric Chavez impolitely greeted McGee with
a single on a soft fly to center, sending Golson racing
to third. Now the visitors had no outs and runners at
first and third. Baseball pundits debate how many
ways there are to score from third base, with some
asserting as many as 18 ways. Hall of Famer Joe
Morgan is said to have named nine ways to score
from third with less than two outs (a hit, a sacrifice
hit, a sacrifice fly, an error, a fielder's choice, a balk, a
wild pitch, a passed ball, a stolen base). Another
observer joked, "Only one way — by crossing home

plate." The Yankees merely needed one of those ways, whether 9 or 18, to regain the lead. Maddon stuck with McGee. Not many others were available, especially considering that the Rays still might have to play a tiebreaker game on Thursday. Enter Jorge Posada, who had remained in the game as Designated Hitter after striking out as a pinch-hitter for Cano in the tenth. Posada, in his last regular-season at bat as a Yankee, ending his seventeenth year (1995-2011) in perhaps a Hall of Fame career, reached first on a fielder's-choice groundout to Longoria, who tagged out Golson unassisted at third. Chavez advanced to second on the play, meaning the Yankees' threat remained: two men on, one out in the top of the twelfth. McGee swung the momentum his way in no-nonsense fashion by striking out Chris Dickerson on three fastballs, recorded at 97, 97, and 98 miles per hour respectively. Boom. Take that. The threat was squashed for good when McGee got Gardner out, a Zobrist-to-Kotchman ground out.

Danger averted, once again. At 11:59 in Baltimore, the Orioles' Nolan Reimold doubled off the Red Sox' Jonathan Papelbon to tie the game at 3. For the bottom of the twelfth at the Trop, Proctor went out to the mound and dispensed with B.J. Upton, striking him out on four fastballs. At midnight the Red Sox stood one out away from extra innings, and Evan Longoria was coming to bat. At 12:02 Robert

Andino's single eluded leftfielder Carl Crawford,
scoring Reimold for an Orioles' victory and Red Sox
defeat, 4-3. The buzz in the crowd was palpable.
Everyone knew what the excitement meant. At worst,
the Rays would play another day. At best, they would
win and ride to the postseason.

Maddon's radio interview relived the "magical
moment." He said, "You knew something really good
was happening in Baltimore regarding us, and it was."
Maddon as well as all Rays fans, far and wide, said, or
prayed, "Come on, Longo."

Proctor served Longoria a fastball for a ball, a slider
for a called strike, and a fastball swing and a miss for
strike two. Longo stepped out when he heard an
elated uproar from the crowd. He then took a fastball
to even the count at 2-2. He fouled a slider off his
shin guard. He looked relaxed but concentrated.
Then on a fastball he lined a rocket to the left field
corner that could not have been lower or faster for
this thirty-first homer, reminiscent of Bobby
Thomson's 1951 liner at the Polo Grounds. Irony of
ironies: the fence there was reportedly lowered to
accommodate former Ray Carl Crawford, to give him
more room to roam, to snag balls. The same Carl
Crawford who just about that moment was skidding
on the grass and just missing the game-winning hit of
the Orioles' Robert Andino. As Rays outfielder Sam

Fuld reported, "The little segment of the Trop's left-field wall, just right of the foul pole looking out from home plate, spans only 20 feet and can't be much more than four feet high. Nobody really knows why it's like that in left field. ... Off the bat, I thought Evan had a sure ground-rule double. It had to be the shortest home run in Tropicana Field history, both in distance and time."

An ecstatic Evan Longoria danced around the bases slamming his helmet off his head as he rounded third, all boyish excitement as he headed home greeted by a sea of Rays. As they celebrated, he smiled and seemed overwhelmed with elation, having to bend over, as if to catch his breath. The Rays had won 8-7 in 12 innings. It was 12:05 a.m.

"That's why baseball is the greatest game," Alex Rodriguez, who did not play in Game 162, told MLB.com after the game. "We're all baseball fans. The emotion of today was something you can't dream up when you make up the schedule."

Ben Bowman @benjbowman
Could anyone have asked for a more exciting way to end the regular season? #MLB

The Rays had captured the American League Wild Card postseason berth after being nine games out on September 4. It was certainly one of the greatest September comebacks in Major League history. "I know it's big," Maddon related to MLB.com after the victory. "I haven't wrapped my mind around it. I haven't grasped it all yet. I will at some point. I'm totally aware of the circumstances and the place in baseball history. But for right now, I'm not quite there yet."

But nearly five months later, speaking to the 620 WDAE town meeting of assembled fans, Tampa Bay Rays Manager Joe Maddon was "there." He knew exactly what he thought. "It was really — everybody I talked to — the best night they've ever seen or had in Major League baseball."

It still doesn't feel real.
Sometimes after the Rays lose, I go to bed and dream that they won.
This is what tonight feels like.
Bwoodrum via DRaysbay.com.

Chapter 12
Rays of Hope

"The universe is made up of stories, not atoms."

Muriel Rukeyser

When "Longoria Happened" for Merrill Frazier in the ear-splitting euphoria of the Trop in St. Pete, Annette Baesel felt its seismic tremors some 5,149 miles away in Italy's Po River Valley, nestled in a rocking chair, awash in the glow of sunrise and Blackberry screen light. How their paths intertwined is a story that crosses borders of age, time, and geography. "Longoria Happened" was the capstone of a week of thrills, in Florida, Italy, cyberspace, and Rays Nation. As for Rays Nation, its nominal president, supreme commander, and high priest is Lenn "Gio" Fraraccio, who serves as a hyper-caffeinated conduit of player information and spiritual energy for fans.

Merrill Frazier, 31 at the time, is a Florida native who grew up in rural country about 30 minutes north of Tampa. He left for the Navy in 1998 (the year the Devil Rays were born) and returned in 2008 (the year the Rays were born). By luck or providence, his exodus coincided with the miserable years of the Tampa franchise and his return home was just in time for their renaissance as perennial contenders in the AL East. A technical trainer for 3D x-ray CT systems, Frazier travels the world teaching technicians and operators how to use these machines.

Annette Baesel, 56 on baseball's starry night, was born and raised in Los Angeles County, a Dodgers fan. She had worked in the environmental planning field in California for a decade before moving north to Seattle for 10 years and eventually settling in the Philadelphia area raising her son, Jason, and becoming active in community work. She and her husband, Jerry, a former investment manager, retired to St. Petersburg in 2010. They became avid Rays fans and season ticket holders. On September 28, 2011, while vacationing in Italy, she had awakened in her Trieste hotel room to bright Adriatic sunlight, hoping it was a good omen for the fortunes of her beloved Rays.

The Rays fans' persona Gio, also known as Giovanni, is 43, with the baseball excitement and innocent enthusiasm of a 13-year-old. Fraraccio (his real-life self) taught history for 13 years and for the last eight years has been selling educational materials to schools. Let's just say his schedule gives him maximum flexibility to all things baseball. He owns some 25,000 baseball cards and a huge autograph collection, but he does not allow himself to either purchase or sell autographs, and his rules are that he must get an autograph on his own and will not accept one if he has not secured it on its own. "Gio" is a frequent caller on WDAE. He wants his ashes buried at the baseball field in Cooperstown.

Young Merrill Frazier played T-ball and Little League, assigned to left field but known as "Mr. Hustle" for his extravagant defensive generosity, with Exhibit A his running past the center fielder to back up the futile efforts of the right fielder. He still prizes the trophy that cited his verve, even though he admits it is "in a box somewhere."

To put into context how the night of September 28, 2011, is enshrined in his memory, Frazier (@MerrillFraz on Twitter) points to the week leading up to it. Through the wonders of social media, he had become attached to cadres of Rays fans he would not have known in more linear, land-line times. One such compadre is our aforementioned Ultimate Fan Gio (@RaysFanGio in Twitter circles). (Lenn tells me he learned the game of baseball by secretly listening late at night in Ohio to Jack Buck and Mike Shannon announcing Cardinals games on the radio. This is another twist of irony to our story: he grew up as a Cardinals fan.) On the eve of the season's final homestand, they sniffed optimism and surprise in the South Florida air and at Gio's urging found themselves at 3 a.m. in the foggy darkness at the local regional airport terminal where the charter flights come in. Gio and another cyber-friend, Dennis Allen, who works at Tropicana Field, had positioned their trucks with a banner taped on one truck and the headlights from the other facing the banner on the access road, but outside of the terminal. Gio had brought a handheld banner that he and his frenzied kids Isabella, 12, and Nicolas, 8, had made (apparently not an unusual thing from this family). The banner was white, with simple blue text in large type that said, "We Believe!!"

They positioned themselves in the line of vision of Rays players and personnel exiting the airport. Rays catcher Kelly Shoppach stopped and rolled down his passenger window and smiled. Several other cars drove by slowly and gave a honk. Then a car slowed up next to the hardy banner-bearing fans, and the passenger rolled down his window. Evan Longoria stuck his head out, pronounced how awesome they were, like a priest providing benediction to the faithful on a pilgrimage to an obscure shrine, and delivered his final blessing, a thumbs-up. Finally as the two charter buses pull through the gate, the pilgrims spot Skipper Joe Maddon, riding in baseball's version of the Popemobile.

As for the final week of the regular season, Merrill Frazier attended nearly all the Rays' home games, even introducing clients from Colombia into his not-so-secret fraternity of fandom. In that span, he brought his son, Austin, his customers, and his uncle from North Carolina. Unfortunately, the one game the Rays lost was the one his son saw, but he had so much fun that it softened the hurt.

Frazier's first "holy-cow magic" moment of the week came on Game 160, on Monday, September 26, attended with his uncle. In a foretaste of the season finale, the Rays staged a comeback, electrifying the hometown crowd at the Trop. The Rays beat the Yankees, 5-2, riding a strong performance from pitcher James Shields (16-12), who missed his twelfth complete game of the season by one out. Kelly Shoppach chipped in with his second homer in as many days. In a mirror image of what would transpire two days later, the Red Sox would lose in Baltimore minutes later, putting Tampa Bay and Boston in a tie for the Wild Card. "Our fate's in our hands now," Shields told MLB.com's Bill Chastain. When the

Rays clubhouse roared in delight at the news from
Baltimore, "I was pleased," Maddon said. "The way
the guys are rallying around this moment -- which
you expect, but they really are -- it's fun to watch."
The fans agreed. "The best part was immediately after
the game," Frazier said. When the stadium's big
screen HD-flashed the in-progress score of the
Orioles-Red Sox game, the Trop burst into high-
decibel bedlam. (Despite assertions to the contrary in
the national media, local denizens insist this ballpark
is indeed very loud when it wants to be.) Then the
place became tensely silent for final moments of the
game in progress against the Yankees. Nobody moved
from their seats. When the Orioles got the final out,
beating the Red Sox 6-3 on the strength of a four-run
sixth inning, the Trop's crew blew the customary
whistle as if the Rays themselves had won another
game -- and the Trop went nuts again.

For the season's penultimate regular-season contest,
Game 161, Frazier took his Colombian customers,
who bore witness to another exciting Rays win. The
Colombians are Rays fans for life.

By the time the calendar turned to September 28, for
the Yankees and Game 162, Merrill Frazier already
found himself exhausted and with barely a voice. He
met up with Gio inside the Trop at the same section
he had been sitting in all week (except the night with

his uncle). It's a small "outcast" section outside of the left-field foul pole. Owing to notoriously sparse attendance, the Trop tends to permit fans the relative luxury of treating seat assignments more like suggestions than rules.

As Frazier recalls, "It's no secret how that game began. To say we were dejected would be a massive understatement. The kids Gio brought, Nicolas and his friend Hunter, were running around the concourse playing their circuit of games one last time and we were left alone to ponder this being the final game of the season. Gio decided it was time to pull out all the superstitious stops. We were moving to 'his spot.' I was kind of honored to find out where this might be. He had mentioned it before, but I had never been there.

"We found the boys (I was there alone), and he told them where he would be and they knew how to find him. In the interest of superstition I'm not going to say where the spot was, but we couldn't see the game live from it but we were able to watch TVs, so we were seeing the Red Sox and the Rays game. Finally, the score got to 7-0 and it was the seventh inning. We knew we were not going to leave the Trop; we were still going to make the most of our last night of 2011 baseball. We decided to go back down and check on his kids again. When we found them, we just stood in the concourse watching them have a good time. I was definitely jealous of the boys — their youthful ignorance was able to enjoy this evening no matter what happened."

Although fans had been trickling out of the ballpark fairly steadily since the fifth inning, Frazier repaired upstairs to sit in the leftfield stands, where he watched the bottom of the seventh and the start of the eighth. Gio texted him, saying he and his crew had gone over behind the Rays bullpen and had a comfy view and were cheering on the pitching crew for fun. So Frazier walked down to them and was watching J.P. Howell loosen up as the Rays ended the top of the eighth.

When the Rays' Johnny Damon singled to the outfield on the second pitch dealt to him, Frazier confessed that he managed a sarcastic "yay!" and a halfhearted clap. But when Ben Zobrist doubled on his first pitch, his cheer volume inched upward. And when Casey Kotchman reached base by getting hit by the pitcher, Frazier and Gio turned to each other and exchanged a look that wordlessly permitted possibility and hope. A new reliever walked pinch-hitter Sam Fuld, stirring the electrons a little more. The banner, which had been folded up securely since the second inning, was suddenly unfurling and being held up. By whom? That's a subplot. Yankees fans seated behind had been cheering for the Rays, because – as every Yankees fan knew – the Rays could put a nail in the coffin of their arch-foes, the Red Sox. The Yankees crew was so excited about the Red Sox losing that they grabbed the banner and unfurled it.

Other Yankees fans, who had been boisterous, started shifting in their seats, but were still confidently jeering and cheering, figuring the Rays would get a run or two and then silently pack their bags until the following February. When Sean Rodriguez received a pass to first as a hit batsman, Frazier and his compatriots began to believe the message of their banner in earnest.

When Frazier and his Colombian customers had come out to the Trop earlier in the week, Gio had taught them all a Longo-related code, a fan idiosyncrasy. When Longo came up to bat, they didn't speak or cheer. They merely displayed three fingers, for his jersey number. For this eighth-inning at-bat, Longo lovers did not have to give the three-fingered salute for long. When Mr. Longoria blasted that home run, everyone knew that the Rays were alive and kicking. Their Wild Card stock had just soared. The boys Gio had brought ran down to the bullpen and held up the banner. The neighboring Rays fans indulged in spirited hugs and hi-fives, and started taunting the Yankees fans, "What's up? We thought this was over!" Curiously, though, Merrill observed more Yankees fans cheering than being silent. He attributes it to a respect for the moment's historical significance — something a Yankees fan, or any other fan, grasped, but not necessarily the partisan who blindly followed a Jeter or an A-Rod, and nothing more.

"The electricity that started the moment Longo connected on that home run was tangible, and it was constant. Pitching changes, inning changes, whatever...the crowd was murmuring at a level that I'd never heard before. Everywhere I turned people were talking excitedly about what was happening. There was life in everyone's eyes that had been absent the entire evening. The night started with something around 29,000 people, and I'd say at this point we had at most 18,000. But it sounded like 40,000," remembered Frazier.

In an era when total victory — The Ring — is the only measure of success, at least one Rays fan saw things from a different perspective. "The eighth inning ended pretty quickly after Longoria's homer, but it didn't matter. Even if the game ended right there, I was satisfied. The feeling that homer gave me was great, and I felt...satisfied," said Frazier, months after the event and even after knowing all that would transpire afterward. I've heard this from other fans in similar circumstances and I've experienced it myself. For example, when I stood for hours by McCovey Cove during Game 1 of the 2010 World Series, I was satisfied. Nothing else mattered. Sure, I wanted ultimate victory, which the Giants did accomplish that year, but at that moment everything – and I mean everything – was fine.

After a quiet top of the ninth, Frazier reported, the Trop started to rumble. Everyone was on their feet when Zobrist came to bat. They all knew what was on the line. "I knew that Boston and Baltimore were in a long weather delay and had been for a while. I knew that we had nothing to lose at this point. Even if we lost, Baltimore was very much into their game and maybe we would still get that playoff."

Frazier continued, "Zobrist and Kotchman went down, and I could feel the wind being sucked out of my chest each out. Then DAN FREAKIN' JOHNSON gets to pinch hit for Sam Fuld. The Great Pumpkin did have a knack for the dramatic. He is the epitome of quality over quantity. He somehow comes up big every time he's in a pivotal situation, and is utterly useless otherwise.

"The home run ball flew right over our heads, and we couldn't even tell it was a home run from our angle until the horn blew and the place erupted. I mean

erupted. I can't even act like I wasn't overcome with
emotion. I had tears for sure and I don't think I was
the only one. We were screaming "WE BELIEVE!"
and others around us were jumping and screaming
and in complete disbelief that we were seeing this," is
how Frazier recounts his eyewitness testimony.

But this was nothing compared to the twelfth inning.
"At the top of the inning we saw that the Red Sox
game had resumed and when we weren't anxiously
staring at the field, we were hawks on the scoreboard.
The problem at this point is that many people with
smart phones were losing battery. I know I had by
this point killed my battery and was trying to save it
for final texts and tweets from family on the status of
the Red Sox game. So for the most part everyone is
just staring at the tiny left-field corner scoreboard,"
according to Merrill Frazier.

He endured a stressful B.J. Upton turn at bat that
seemed endless. Merrill had once witnessed an Upton
walk-off and surmised that Upton would be the
prime candidate for hero status on this night. But
when Upton fanned, Frazier concluded that this
would not be the inning. His own words of what
happened next retain the immediacy and freshness of
Evan Longoria at the plate: "Longoria comes to bat
and the crowd loses its mind. He gets more cheers
than anyone to begin with, but tonight nothing was

subtle, the Trop NEEDED him to do it again. His last HR was still very much on my mind. He crushed that one, and I thought for sure he was going to press too much. His first few pitches kind of affirmed that...then something started to happen.

"It started with a rumbling throughout the crowd. Some people started talking excitedly. I heard a 'whoop' here and there, and of course the first thing Gio and I assume is that Boston lost...but we had no way to confirm it. Everyone is frantically searching the crowd, the scoreboards, anything for confirmation...but for 15 agonizing seconds nothing happened.

"Then the executive suite below the press box explodes, and like 'the wave' the news spreads like wildfire throughout the stands. But still, we were too scared to believe it until they updated the scoreboard. And when they did the score said, 'Boston 3, Baltimore 4...FINAL' it was better than anything yet. Longoria's first homer, Johnson's homer with two outs, two strikes, at the bottom of the ninth, none of that was as exhilarating (yet) as this. I knew the season wasn't over no matter what and the Trop exploded in the middle of Longoria's at-bat. I think I remember him stepping out of the box and asking for a timeout, and I saw the Yankees defense looking around at the crowd almost as if to say, 'Yeah, we get it.' I swear it still seems like it wasn't real, like we were in some corny, scripted Hollywood movie. Right there, I knew this was going to be a historic night, no matter what happened next.

"Then...Longoria happened. When he first made contact, from our angle it looked foul right away. I didn't even see Longoria running to first, I was staring too hard at the ball. I saw it hit the Crawford Corner and bounce around and since I had sat there I knew there was almost no path for a fair ball to land there. Then the horn blew and for a half-second I didn't believe it. I just looked at Gio and the kids and felt the slaps on my back from the fans behind us that we had been sharing the extra innings with and just...stopped. All the cliché stuff about time standing still, about hearing nothing, all I could do is stare at the spot that Longoria's ball just hit...then I lost it. What little was left of my voice was gone before Longoria even hit third base. Luckily, Gio had some sense, while the crowd was still cheering and screaming and crying, he was gathering me and the kids up and we were bee-lining for the Rays dugout. He was determined to be part of the celebration.

"We got to the rail just in time for everyone else to realize that's where they wanted to be. Myself and some random other fan unfurled the 'WE BELIEVE!!' banner and just held it up for an eternity.

My arms were so sore, but I didn't care. We watched
the news crews and the team chatting and hugging
and interviewing and we were a part of it all.
Eventually the bubbly came out, and who else to start
it but David Price. He starts spraying all of us then
his eyes catch Gio. He stops, looks at him, and says,
'Oh man....youuuu!' and proceeds to pour the rest of
it on Gio's head. I high-fived Fuld and got to bear-
hug Peralta as he jumped into the crowd."

•   •   •

Annette Baesel's earliest memories of baseball were
listening to Dodgers games on the radio. Her father
passed away when she was 12, so most of her
memories of that time revolve around her father's
brother, her Uncle Bob. These were the Dodgers of
Don Drysdale, Sandy Koufax, Jim Lefebvre, and
Willie Davis. "I remember my dad and my
grandmother playing 'woofle ball' with me in the
backyard. I was never very good, but I loved the time
spent with them," Annette related. She also recalled
the 1967 math teacher, also the middle school boys
baseball coach, who permitted his students "quiet
work" while they got to listen to the final game of the
World Series on radio.

As a Seattle Mariners fan in 1995, Baesel took her
son, Jason, to Game 5 of the Mariners-Yankees

American League Division Series. The 57,411
spectators packed into the Kingdome were so loud
she and her son wore earplugs as the hometowners
prevailed 6-5 with two runs in the bottom of the
ninth to take the ALDS. Future Hall of Famer
Randy Johnson got the win.

When the Baesels moved to the Philadelphia area in
2000, they naturally adopted the Phillies but followed
mostly via newspaper and TV. Arena football
captured much of their attention as fans. In 2007, the
Baesels moved to St. Petersburg, where they bought a
historic home to renovate and expand. For three years,
they worked on approvals, planning, and construction.
During that time, they periodically rented a small,
furnished apartment. The owners, Tom Wiemken,
his wife Els, and son, Pieter, were Rays fans
extraordinaire. Once Tom, a longtime Rays season
ticket holder, invited Jerry Baesel to a game, and
Annette and Jerry were hooked. They bought season
tickets one section over from Tom (Section 301 Row
D, seats 7 and 8) and joined the fraternity of Sections
300/301/302. (Tom died in a tragic accident in
December 2010, but his family carries on their
tradition as Rays season ticket holders.) Annette and
Jerry typically attend about two-thirds of the Rays
home games, giving the rest to friends or neighbors.

Annette Baesel is a knowledgeable fan, reading the
sports page daily during the season and following on
Twitter a host of Rays players, manager Joe Maddon,
DJ Kitty, and a lively circle of Rays fans and sports
reporters. As @abaesel2, she often Tweets live from
Rays games, exchanging real-time, on-the-scene
reactions and observations to her nearly 2,000 Twitter
followers.

Recalls Annette Baesel: "My husband Jerry and I flew
to Italy on September 21 for a month's slow travel on
the back roads of Italy. We had found happy homes
for tickets for the games we knew we'd miss and
crossed our fingers that we'd have postseason games
to follow via Twitter and MLB.com. All but one of
the regular season games were at 7:10 ET, so I knew
I'd only get the morning 'recap' by going back
through my Twitter stream to catch the highlights.
Of course, when we left we only had a small glimmer
of hope to make the playoffs."

But each day as they drove through the Dolomites
and the Friuli region of northeastern Italy, the hope
persisted. "We woke up on a bright sunny fall day in
Trieste on the twenty-eighth realizing that that
glimmer of hope was almost as bright as the sun
shining on the Adriatic Sea outside of our hotel room.
That day we drove south from Trieste to the Po River

Valley for a four-day stay at Le Occare, an agriturismo (farm stay) in a rural area outside Ferrara."

Le Occare is a 68-acre farm that has been in the same family for at least three generations. Once a hemp and tobacco farm, it boasts acres of nut trees now tended more for truffles. The owners also grow vegetables, herbs, and berries in a kitchen garden, have an apple orchard, fields of corn and soybean, and make their own honey from their own bees and hives.

The B&B is a two-story ancestral stone farmhouse covered by vines and surrounded by pomegranate bushes, oaks, and is home to a lovely bunch of truffle-hunting hounds. The home is charming with stone floors, thick walls, heavy doors, yellow walls, floor-to-ceiling book shelves topped with a collection of old stoneware pots, and a huge welcoming kitchen.

"We arrived at Le Occare, late in the afternoon on the twenty-eighth. After a short walk, an introduction to the dogs, and a nap, we settled down to a spectacular dinner served on old family china and linens. A big dinner and a bit of wine after a long day's drive did not bode well for the idea of staying up to follow the game in the middle of the night. But I was determined to get at least the first few innings. So I read until 1 a.m., when the game started. But after several innings of 'watching' David Price struggle and no Rays runs and a strong Yankee pitcher, I decided to just catch the recap in the morning…with coffee," noted Annette in an e-mail.

"Just before 4 a.m. I woke up for a wander to the WC. I thought, 'Should check the final score,' figuring the game would be over and the Rays would be headed home for the winter. As I got out of bed, I saw the game was still going with a score of 7-3, but groggily I figured we were still going home. Just a few minutes later on my way back to bed, my Twitter stream exploded as Evan Longoria hit the three-run home run and the score was now 7-6. So there I stood in the middle of a darkened room in my cotton nightie and with bare feet on a cold stone floor saying to myself, 'Well, I can't go back to sleep now.'

"So I sat down on the rocker in the corner of the room, shivering just a bit, to follow the game a bit more. I held my breath through the top of the ninth as the Yankees went scoreless. Then we were up again, out 1, out 2….I'm beginning to think I'll get back in bed where it's warm for the last out. Then I see that Dan Johnson is up to bat and there is a collective groan across the Twitterverse. With a sigh of resignation, I definitely decide to head back to the warmth of the blankets. And BAM….my Twitter stream explodes for the second time of the night as Dan Johnson hits the homer that ties the game.

Hubby woke up on that one, because, no, I just couldn't keep silent.

"Jerry rolls over to look at me with that resigned look only 26 years of marriage could produce as he sees me sitting up in bed staring intently at the screen on my Blackberry. 'What's up?' he asks. 'We're tied 7 -7 in the ninth,' I say. 'Wow, what time is it?' he mumbles as he rolls back over."

Baesel retreated to the corner of the room in the rocker, bathed in Blackberry screen light, now with socks on and wrapped in a blanket, determined to follow to the end, bitter or sweet, the contest playing out six time zones away. She digitally followed play by play, Tweet by Tweet, tensely surviving the tenth and eleventh innings, buoyed by the camaraderie of her Rays community back in the U.S.A.

"There was a lot of breath holding, and rocking....lots of rocking. And then, there was Evan...again. Finding it hard to believe lightning was going to strike twice, I kept rocking figuring we were going to see the thirteenth inning."

Then Twitter displayed a mini-eruption as the rain-delayed Red Sox lost, and Annette and her legions realized that even if the Tampa Bay Rays suffered a lost despite the gallant comeback, they would still get one more chance in a game against the Bosox. "A few minutes later for the THIRD time in the middle of my night, my Twitter stream exploded like fireworks on the 4th of July. We had won on a home run by Evan Longoria. Once again a squeal escaped my lips and Jerry once again rolled over asking, 'What happened?' We won, we won, we won!

"As I climbed back into bed, the sky was starting to lighten over the fields of the Po River Valley. Birds were rustling in the bushes outside my windows, and I could hear the stirring of the truffle dogs."

•   •   •

Stateside, if any truffle dogs were stirring, Lenn "Gio" Fraraccio could not hear them because the roar in his head after Longoria Happened was still too loud. Sleep was not in the realm of the possible. "I droppped off Hunter at 2:30. I talked to his parents for 15 minutes, and got home at 3 a.m. I watched MLB network and watched baseball stuff on the computer. Then I noticed my favorite radio show was on at 6 a.m. I listened for 30 minutes. Then I called and sang 'Red Sox Decline.'"

Gio provided the following words of the chorus of a taunting parody of "Sweet Caroline," an anthem of Red Sox World Series years:

Red Sox decline O O O
Longo hit the ball over the small wall.
Red Sox decline O O O
Carl Crawford dropped the ball. Y'all !!!

He continued his post-victory winding-down chronicle: "Then I left the house. Got Mountain Dew five-hour energy. Then I went to two schools because I had to train them. Then I called my buddy Dennis, and went to his house. We made banners and drove to the airport to wish the guys good luck on their way to Texas. They left about 2-3 p.m. Then I went home and crashed around 5 p.m."

Such are the wages of winning.

"This moment contains all moments."

C.S. Lewis

Epilogue
Full Circle

"We shall not cease from exploration
And the end of all our exploring
Will be to arrive where we started
And know the place for the first time."

T.S. Eliot, "Little Gidding"

What just happened here? Sure, four baseball games
decided who the Wild Card winners would be in
2011. Though we did not talk about it, other matters
in the baseball world were in play on September 28:
home-field advantages, Division Series matchups,
batting titles, individual accomplishments for the
record books, attendance records, and on and on. To
some who follow baseball — and many who do not
follow sports at all — the matters at hand were ho-
hum, a few blips on the screen of a Wednesday
evening's diversions and distractions. To others,
baseball fans or not, some of what we experienced

through the prism of baseball that evening and early morning felt different — not that we have to dress it up and call it something fancy. But during and after the events, many of us said or thought, "Wow! What was that all about?"

First, the down-to-earth matters (some of which were yet again a bit off-the-ground). The long-shot St. Cardinals continued their improbable path and went on to win the World Series in 2011. After beating Houston 8-0, coupled with Atlanta's 4-3 13-inning loss to the Phillies, the Redbirds possessed the qualities of that overused word "momentum," only they italicized and boldfaced it and came up with a brand-new font for it. In the National League Division Series, or NLDS, which the victory on Baseball's Starry Night enabled the Cards to enter, the Cardinals upended and ousted the National League Eastern Division winners, the Phillies, who had won a record 102 games. Meeting each other in the postseason for the first time, the teams battled in a five-game series, with the favored Phillies enjoying home-field advantage. The Phillies had clinched their division back on September 17 and ended with the best record in all of baseball. Before 46,480 fans at Citizens Bank Park in Philadelphia, the Cardinals jumped on starter Roy Halladay in the first inning with a Lance Berkman three-run homer. But the Phillies prevailed, 11-6, beating Kyle Lohse and riding on the strength of homers by Ryan Howard and Raul Ibanez. The Cardinals took Game 2 with a 5-4 score, defeating 2008 American League Cy Young winner Cliff Lee. Although the Phillies were the ones with the early 4-0 lead against Chris Carpenter, pitching on three days' rest, the Cards scored three in the fourth, on RBIs from Ryan Theriot, Jon Jay, and Rafael Furcal, and tied the game in the sixth on a Jay single. They took the lead on an Albert Pujols single in the seventh and their bullpen held off the Phillies with six innings of scoreless one-hit pitching. Octavio Dotel secured the win and Jason Motte got a four-out save. With the series moving to Busch Stadium in St. Louis, the visitors notched a 3-2 win and 2-1 edge in the NLDS in a tense pitchers' duel — the Phils' Cole Hamels and the Cards Jaime Garcia each pitching six scoreless innings. A pinch home run by Ben Francisco gave the Phillies a 3-0 lead, which they clung to despite a pair of St. Louis runs and scoring threats right to the end. Game 4, played before 47,071 at Busch, the second-largest crowd in the stadium's history, went to the Cards, 5-3, to even the series. To those inclined to believe baseball superstition, the antics of a so-called rally squirrel were instrumental in Roy Oswalt's loss and the Cards' win. In the fifth inning, a squirrel crossed the plate as Oswalt was ready to deliver a pitch to Skip Schumaker. It was called a ball, although the Phils' Charlie Manuel and company argued for a call of "no pitch." The Cards were already leading 3-2 and the incident did not affect the outcome, but the hometown fans and media now had a new story angle. For the deciding Game 5 back in Philly, a matchup between the game's top hurlers lived up to its billing. Chris Carpenter beat Roy Halladay, 1-0, on a three-hit shutout, allowing a Rafael Furcal triple and Skip Schumaker double in the first to stand up. The game was a throwback, with Halladay tossing 126 pitches and Carpenter working out of jams to go the distance.

The Cardinals also took the ensuing best-of-seven National League Championship Series, or NLCS, four games to two, against the NL Central champion Milwaukee Brewers, who had defeated the NL West champion Arizona Diamondbacks in the NLCS. This "Suds Series," so named because both teams had strong links, including ballpark names, to beer brewers, featured a 9-6 Brewers' win in Game 1, with home runs from Ryan Braun, Prince Fielder, and Yuniesky Betancourt. St. Louis roared back with a 17-hit attack and 12-3 win in the second game, at Miller Park, with round trippers from Albert Pujols and David Freese. Games 3, 4, and 5 were played in St. Louis, with the Cardinals taking two of three and an NLCS lead of 3-2. Carpenter and the Cards won Game 3 by 4-3, and the Brewers staved off a 3-1 NLCS hole with a 4-2 Game 4 Randy Wolf win. In Game 5, St. Louis brought Milwaukee to the edge

with a 7-1 win aided by four Brewer errors. The
Cardinals gained their third trip to the World Series
in eight years, having won it all as recently as 2006,
against the Detroit Tigers, with a 12-6 trouncing of
the Brewers in Milwaukee.

The "We've Come a Long Way, Baby!" Cardinals
won the 2011 World Series in seven games against
the returning Texas Rangers. The World Series is
best remembered for two things: three home runs by
the soon-to-be departing Albert Pujols in Game 3
and a scintillating roller-coaster ride in Game 6.
Pujols's three clouts in a 16-7 lambasting of Texas
matched a World Series feat accomplished by only
two others, Babe Ruth twice, in 1926 and 1928, and
Reggie Jackson, in 1977. Pujols also tied a record for
most hits (5) and most RBIs (6) in a World Series
game while setting a record for total bases (14). And
the Game 6 heroics, book-worthy in their own right,
put the brightest spotlight on young David Freese,
the Cardinals third baseman. Twice in the game the
Rangers edged within one strike of winning, which
would have landed them their first World Series
trophy. Freese's clutch hitting was pivotal and historic.
In the bottom of the ninth inning, his two-out, two-
strike triple drove in two runs to tie the score at 7.
Each team put up two runs in the tenth inning.
Freese's walk-off homer in the eleventh won the
game, 10-9, and the Cardinals finished the job the

next day in Game 7, by a 6-2 score, in St. Louis
behind — who else? — Chris Carpenter. Freese
earned — an understatement — World Series MVP
honors, and his 21 RBIs in the 2011 postseason set a
record.

The aftermath of the Cardinals' triumphant offseason
saw radical changes: Tony La Russa retired after
being at the helm in St. Louis since 1996 (replaced by
Mike Matheny) and Albert Pujols leaving town for
the Los Angeles Angels of Anaheim, evidently more
lured by the Angels' offer of $240 million for 10 years
than long-time ties to St. Louis. La Russa's
managerial career stretched from 1979 through 2011,
with stints with the Chicago White Sox and Oakland
A's preceding his time in St. Louis with the National
League. His teams won six pennants and three World
Series.

The Phillies, with their second-ranked $173-million
2011 payroll (according to The Associated Press),
would not represent the only big-money collapse in
the postseason. Forlorn Red Sox fans ($161.4-million
payroll, ranked, third according to AP) would find a
small measure of solace in the New York Yankees',
payroll of $201.7 million (highest), fall to the Detroit
Tigers in the American League Division Series, 3-2.
The dramatic series included two record-setting
crowds (Game 5: 50,960, which surpassed 50,940 in

Game 1) at the recently rebuilt Yankee Stadium. Rain was an added player in the first game, forcing a suspension in the second inning, with play resumed the next day. In that contest, the Bronx Bombers bombed their way to a 9-3 win against the Tigers, but in Game 2 the visitors from the Motor City won 5-3, led by starter Max Scherzer who hurled no-hit ball for 5.1 innings. Game 3 at Comerica Park went to the Tigers, 5-4, with 2011 American League Cy Young unanimous winner Justin Verlander (24 wins, 250 strikeouts) besting CC Sabathia. Behind the sometimes-banished and inconsistent A.J. Burnett, the Yankees creamed the Tigers in Game 4, 10-1. But in a rare postseason, season-ending loss at home, the Yankees succumbed to the Tigers, 3-2, when closer Jose Valverde got his fifty-first consecutive save of 2011, including the postseason, by striking out Alex Rodriquez.

As for our two teams who suffered historic collapses that climaxed on September 28, the Atlanta Braves' aftershocks were the most muted. The Braves fired hitting coach Larry Parrish two days after that fateful night. This was not altogether shocking, given the Braves' paltry offense epitomized by scoring seven runs in the team's last five games of 2011, all losses. Atlanta opted for stability, signing contracts with the likes of pitchers Jair Jurrjens, Eric O'Flaherty, Brandon Beachy, Jonny Venters, Tommy Hanson,

Craig Kimbrel, Cristhian Martinez, and Kris Medlen;
infielders Freddie Freeman and Jack Wilson; and
outfielders Martin Prado, Jason Heyward, and
Michael Bourn. "Adding by subtracting," in the eyes
of many Braves fans, the team allowed starter Derek
Lowe and reliever Scott Linebrink to depart.

Boston was another story. The upheaval was swift.
Terry Francona and the Red Sox parted ways after
eight years (2004-11) and two World Championships.
The split was a messy divorce with leaks and
accusations of a lost clubhouse and personal issues.
The house cleaning reached the upper ranks of the
front office, with General Manager Theo Epstein
departing for the Chicago Cubs. The spillage over all
was indelicate and acrimonious with fans and local
media second-guessing and replaying the agonies of
the 2011 season. The Red Sox hired former Texas
Rangers and Mets manager Bobby Valentine, who
was popular and successful in a stint as manager in
Japan, as Francona's replacement. Another radical
change for the Red Sox involved the departure of
closer Jonathan Papelbon, for Philadelphia (four years,
for $50 million). In his seven years with the Bosox,
Papelbon racked up 219 saves, with another seven
saves in the postseason. His meltdown on September
28, 2011, was his last appearance for Boston.

And what of the Tampa Bay Rays, the team and the fans who stood at the top of the mountain minutes after midnight on September 28, 2011? The Rays never got a sure grasp on that rippling "Momentum" banner that the Cardinals paraded. Meeting the Texas Rangers in the ALDS for the second consecutive year, Joe Maddon's Rays managed only one postseason win, losing the series 3-1. Reminiscent of the New York Giants in 1951 after Bobby Thomson's famous home run, the Rays may have emptied their emotional bank accounts via their September charge. Such speculation is risky; plus, it does a disservice to the ALDS winners, the Texas Rangers. The facts are that Tampa showed plenty of something — call it "momentum" or anything you want — in Game 1, in Arlington, Texas, blasting three homers (one by Johnny Damon and two by Kelly Shoppach) on the way to a 9-0 drubbing of Texas. Most remarkably, Rays' rookie starter Matt Moore, 22, shut down the Rangers' vaunted offense, allowing no runs, two hits, and two walks while striking out six in seven innings. It was Moore's second Major League start. But the Rangers took Game 2, 8-6, courtesy of a five-run fourth that overcame a three-run deficit. Starter James Shields took the loss. Wednesday's hero Evan Longoria launched a three-run shot in the seventh, to bring Tampa within a run of Texas, but it was not enough. Back at the Trop in Game 3, Texas held on to win 4-

3 as Colby Lewis outdueled David Price. Two solo home runs by Tampa's Desmond Jennings were not enough. The Rangers' Mike Napoli had a two-run homer. The Texas Rangers sailed into the ALCS for the second year in a row, winning 4-3 in ALDS Game 4, their fifth straight postseason win in the Rays' house, largely on the strength of Adrian Beltre's three homers.

In a further postscript for the Rays, the Baseball Writers' Association of America voted Joe Maddon the 2011 American League Manager of the Year for guiding a team that had started the season 0-6 into the postseason. (He also won the award in 2008.) The Tampa Bay Rays extended Maddon's contract for three years in February 2012. As for two other stars of September, Dan Johnson became a free agent and signed a minor league contract with the Chicago White Sox, and Evan Longoria looked to improve his performance offensively and defensively as the Rays' popular third baseman, affectionately known as "Longo." The Rays also signed rookie Matt Moore to a five-year $14-million contract.

The most significant aftermath of 2011 was the new playoff format that Major League Baseball and the players union agreed to in March 2012. Starting in 2012, Major League Baseball expanded its postseason playoff format to 10 teams, adding a second Wild

Card team in each league. In doing so, MLB set up a new playoff round consisting of a play-in game between the teams with the best records who are not division winners. Under this scenario, a third-place team could advance and eventually win the World Series. The move was not without controversy, from players and fans alike, but it resulted from a new Basic Agreement announced November 22, 2011. The agreement stipulated that the postseason would expand no later than 2013.

In a statement, MLB Commissioner Bud Selig said, "The enthusiasm for the 10-team structure among our clubs, fans, and partners has been overwhelming. This change increases the rewards of a division championship and allows two additional markets to experience playoff baseball each year, all while maintaining the most exclusive postseason in professional sports."

His counterpart, Michael Weiner, the executive director of the Major League Baseball Players Association, said: "The players are eager to begin playing under this new format in 2012, and they look forward to moving to full realignment in 2013. Our negotiating committee and the owners' representatives worked hard to develop a schedule that should make for fairer competition and provide our fans with a very exciting season."

Did you catch that word "realignment"? As part of the Basic Agreement, the Houston Astros move to the American League in 2013, equalizing the National League and American League at 15 teams each with each league maintaining three divisions. The Houston Astros, featured in our first-game spotlight devoted to September 28, can claim the most radical team overhaul of all the participants in this drama. You've all heard of the "player to be named later," abbreviated as PTBNL in fan circles. This is more or less the "team to be named later," or TTBNL, in a trade from one league to the other.

What does all this mean?

The story you just read can never happen again.

Granted, that is always the case, just as no two baseball games have ever been exactly the same, nor will they ever be — not even, say, two perfect games. It would be mathematically possible theoretically, but not in the arena of human affairs. The same as chess. Or any other game in any other sport, to give them their due. But if additional Wild Card teams were in the mix in 2011, the Atlanta Braves and the Boston Red Sox would have had one more chance to stave off their historic collapses, one more chance to win. Who knows? They could have met each other in the World Series!

The pros and cons of this revised playoff format will be debated and discussed on Internet message boards, blogs, and other fan forums, as well as in newspaper columns, on sports-talk radio, and on cable sports networks.

My view? I am ambivalent but open-minded. At heart, I am a purist who would not mind all that much if MLB and the MLBPA reverted to the postseason regime that was in place from 1903-68, when there were no divisions and the two pennant winners went straight to the World Series. Pure. Clean. Simple. But that is sentimental nostalgia and silly. Besides, there was no players' union for many of those years, at least not one with any power. And turning the clock back like that also sends us to the world of segregated baseball and other injustices. Our sepia-toned memories sometimes demand closer inspection. Nevertheless, I worry that the revised format is a slippery slope that will inevitably lead Major League Baseball to formats like other professional sports. Pretty soon, nearly every team will qualify for the postseason, sort of like getting an honor roll certificate just for showing up at school. Speaking of going retro, part of the solution involves returning to a 154-game schedule, but that is not ever likely to happen: too much revenue at stake.

Of course, I have selfish reasons for resisting a change in the playoff format. After all, why mess with a scheme that enabled me, as well as you, to experience the twists and turns and surprises of September 28, 2011? Why would we want to tinker further with the cosmos? We should be engaging in deep bows of gratitude to the gods and goddesses of baseball who ordained or permitted the clockwork pulleys to move as they did. (All due respect to those who were pained by the results.)

In 1991, the music critics David Hajdu and Roy Hemming wrote, "The day Frank Sinatra dies the 20th century is over." (Sinatra died May, 14, 1998.) Naturally, they were referring to matters far beyond the calendar on the wall. What is the baseball version of that statement? For me, it's easy. "The day Willie Mays dies the 20th century is over." What about after that? When did baseball's 21st century begin? One can make a strong argument for September 28, 2011. It certainly was not the only night in baseball history with a "did you see that?" quality. And it definitely cannot claim it was the only exciting night for players and spectators alike. But the events of that evening were connected in ways that were impossible in 1951 or 1986 or 2001. Social networking sites like Facebook and Twitter enabled fans to create and nurture communities that could not exist — never mind thrive — a few short years ago. Not bound by geography or age or ballpark presence, fans connected and commented, in real time as events unfurled. They were able to lick each other's wounds in mourning or soak up cyber-Champagne with their fellow fans. Even players became fans. With today's virtual-world gateways and portals, fans and players have a link they never had before.

And that has been the reward for me. About midway through this effort, I pivoted. I discovered that all the tension and loss and triumph (and everything in between) are created, yes, by the games themselves and the players who perform under such intense pressure with such power and grace. Yet, after being privileged to experience the moving stories of my "secret sharers" — fans who were at the games, and fans who were not — I shifted the narrative from the games and players to the fans and their stories, their deeply personal journeys. These were individuals with busy lives who could not wait to tell us about something "felt in the blood, and felt along the heart," in the words of William Wordsworth. And that something is baseball.

Acknowledgments

I am grateful for all those who helped me to get information and for those who supported me in myriad other ways, known and unknown to them. My friend Greg Tobin served as motivator, coach, sounding board, navigator, and father confessor. Having written and edited many books over the years, he was able to tell me how and when to stand in the batter's box for this effort. Then there are the fans, who are the heart of the book. Their stories moved me, and I thank them for their time, their openness, their honesty — and their own voices. I owe a special note to Michael Kruse of the *Tampa Bay Times*. His article of that night, when it was the *St. Petersburg Times*, written with Ben Montgomery, gave me a spark, and a conversation with Kruse led me to the Tampa fans. It transformed my approach, for the better. I am indebted to the fans who told me their stories, whether the retelling got in here or not. My thanks to Bill Lee, for a lively conversation filled with unique perspectives that got me to think in new ways. Thanks also to Lenn Fraraccio especially for connecting me to local resources and story lines I was not aware of. The fans in the book deserve a deep bow from me. All the folks whose stories you just read in the preceding chapters get a hearty hug from me. I look forward to seeing you at games, virtually or otherwise. A supporting cast of fans and supporters in no perfect order includes Len Berman, Doris Kearns Goodwin, Jayson Stark, Bob Netherton, Becky and Roger Bayne, Dan Valenti, Mark Murphy, Steve and Tracie Boudreau, Tom Coman, Mike McCormick, Pete Covert, Paul Silvia, Jim Morrison, Charlie Selden, Bob Mitchell, Susan Horvath Hundt, Bob Shearer, Mary Church, David O'Brien, Andrew Heydt, Bob Beghtol, Tim Hayes, Warren Young, James Bresnahan, Ian Hussey, Joe Bergin, David and Laurie Choplinski, Gary Velez, Ken Wagner, Craig Vaughn, Steve Melikean, Michael Scott, Ted Speros, Jan Wessel, Peter MacInerney, Rege Behe, and anyone else whose name escapes me at this moment. Any omission is clumsiness on my part owing to the frenzy of getting this book out in the most timely fashion. For any one not listed, I beg your indulgence and understanding.

My agent James Fitzgerald has been diligent and energetic in making sure this project saw the light of day. I thank him for his advocacy and professionalism. I am indebted to author Michael Streissguth for connecting me to him.

Finally, my brother Bob Kocak was instrumental in connecting me to Bill Lee and other sports luminaries. I thank him for his superb networking and belief in this book. Jack Kocak is the brother who played ball with me in the backyard. We are good friends and treasure that weekly Skype. My late half-brother Thomas R. Hayes inspired me by telling me about Willie Mays, and that began it all. Our mom, Josephine Kocak, at 95, inspires every single day. My son Ethan Kocak cannot be thanked enough for the work of art he created for the cover. My daughter Evelyn Kocak has offered constant encouragement and support to keep me en pointe, and my daughter Adrianna Kocak, the most baseball-oriented of all my children, gets me to "buck up" and offers simpatico companionship as a fan. Most of all, I could not have undertaken this book without the support of my wife, Beth, on a gazillion practical levels. She believed when I doubted, and was always positive and hopeful about this project. Thanks. A final expression of gratitude to all who have bought and read this book — and have read this far.

Made in the USA
Charleston, SC
10 May 2012